STRATEGIC MANAGEMENT IN CONSTRUCTION

STRATEGIC MANAGEMENT IN CONSTRUCTION

David Langford
and
Steven Male

Gower

Published by
Gower Publishing Company Limited
Gower House
Croft Road
Aldershot
Hants GU11 3HR
England

Gower Publishing Company
Old Post Road
Brookfield
Vermont 05036
USA

British Library Cataloguing in Publication Data
Langford, D.A.
  Strategic management in Construction.
  1. Construction industries. Management
  I. Title II. Male, Steven
  624.068

  ISBN 0–566–09015–5

Phototypeset by Input Typesetting Ltd, London
Printed in Great Britain by
Billing & Sons Ltd, Worcester

Contents

Figures

Tables

Preface

Strategy is a subject that has exercised the minds of political, military and business leaders for centuries. The earliest recorded attempts to define strategy emanate from Roman military commanders who sought to document the strategic options available on the battlefield. Although we hope that the need for military strategy based around combat will continue to decline in response to a changed pattern of international relations, the need to apply strategy to business organizations is widely recognized. The acceptance of the need for strategic behaviour in business is evidenced by the volume of literature dedicated to the subject. Much of the knowledge base has been developed by researchers and theorists; practitioners have had to apply critical judgements on how such theories can be applied to their own industry. This is particularly so in the construction industry where little material in the strategic management field has been available, despite the efforts of authors such as Newcombe, Channon and Grinyer who have done much to bring strategic management theories to the attention of practising construction managers.

This book attempts to bring together such work so that degree students and those studying for professional qualifications, as well as practitioners, can develop their knowledge of strategic management and how it is applied in construction. The book covers four aspects of the subject: the construction context; the theory of strategy; the techniques for applying strategy; and the mechanics of how strategy is formulated. The context is set by brief discussions of the nature of the construction environment and how construction organizations (be they contractors or consultants) operate within this environment. These contributions do not seek to replicate other worthy analyses of the construction industry structure. They do not fully atomize and describe the workings of the industry; the intention is merely to set the scene for the later sections of the book. The theory of strategy is dealt with in two parts – the first reviews the general theory and the second comments on how this theory fits a construction setting. The theoretical discussion is followed by an examination of some of the techniques that strategic planners may use. Some of these techniques are highly mathematical and may involve the use of statistics. However, the text is not swamped with numerical analysis and we hope that the strategic planner will recognize when mathematical analysis is required and arrange for the appropriate expert advice. The final section of the book deals with the mechanics of how strategy is formulated taking, as case studies, five contracting firms and three professional practices. The intention is to offer insights into the way in which other firms have introduced strategic thinking into their organizations for managers in construction.

The book concludes with a chapter which synthesizes the theory and the practice, thereby creating a model for managers to follow. This model does not claim to be prescriptive but sets out a methodology which practitioners can use in their own construction organizations.

The writing of this book has proved a valuable experience for us and we hope that the reader will similarly benefit from it. The product is, however, the work of many and the contribution of Jill Pearce at Gower in the form of encouragement and patience needs to be acknowledged as does that of Elaine Winter for her editorial contribution. Students and colleagues have also contributed to our thinking and we gratefully acknowledge their efforts.

Dave Langford, Bath
Steve Male, Edinburgh

Acknowledgements

The authors wish to acknowledge the senior personnel in construction companies and professional practices who freely gave of their time to enable case studies to be prepared.

Figures 3.2 and 9.1 are adapted with permission of The Free Press, a division of Macmillan, Inc. from *Competitive Strategy, Techniques for Analyzing Industries and Competitors*, by Michael E. Porter. Copyright © 1980 by The Free Press.

Thanks also go to Beverly Harding for her painstaking efforts in the preparation of the manuscript.

Introduction

This book is about strategy for construction organizations. Strategy may exist at a number of levels in an organization. Corporate stragegy, for example, concerns decisions about the organization as a whole and includes acquisition and divestment decisions. On the other hand business strategy is about how an organization should compete in a particular market, for example, house building, engineering and property development. At a third level organizations will have operational or project strategies which concern decisions made by the individual department head or project manager, such as estimating, buying and plant purchase, which influence the performance of the firm as a whole. This book focuses on corporate and business strategy and the process of strategic decision-making.

In construction organizations managers have to make decisions about the strategic direction of their organization be they contractors or people associated with the design process. Senior managers will be concerned about the scope of an organization's activities, for example, what services should we provide to our customers? For contractors such decisions could revolve around the systems of procurement to be offered to clients or, more fundamentally, the type of construction markets to enter and the geographical regions of the country (or the world) in which the firm is to operate. Other strategic decisions could focus upon the kind of forward or backward integration that a firm wishes to enjoy. Forward integration could involve establishing property companies to find sites which the construction division could then develop for the property side to present to the property market. Alternatively a construction firm could backwardly integrate by buying up suppliers of material or key subcontractors. In professional practices strategic decisions could similarly relate to the professional services offered to clients and one forward integrating mechanism would be to offer professional construction management or project management services. An illustration of backward integration would be the purchase of a firm of computer experts working on computer-aided design. (CAD)

Such strategic decisions will define the boundary of the organization. This boundary is the point of contact between the firm and the external environment and strategic decisions can shift this boundary. For example, a firm may take a strategic decision to offer a design and build service, something that was previously outside the scope of the organization. Thus the boundary of the organization is extended to encompass this new development.

The concept of 'environment' needs further consideration. In the late 1980s this word was widely used and can encompass references as diverse as the stratosphere or the street corner. In this text environment is used to describe the context of the construction industry. This includes the political, social, economic and psychological factors which shape the prospects for the industry. The construction environment is volatile and the construction industry may prosper or be severely affected by relatively small changes in that environment. Small shifts in the interest rate, for example, may sharply influence the house-buying behaviour of individuals or the development intentions of important clients.

The task of the strategic planner in a construction organization is to synchronize the organization's activities with those of the construction environment. Clearly this process must be consistent with the resources of the firm; there is little point in a small builder setting a strategic objective of becoming involved in tunnelling work if the builder cannot gain access to the large amounts of capital required to enable him to access this market. Strategic decisions are frequently complex because the environment is frequently uncertain and, moreover, decisions taken will influence the long-term direction of the organization.

So, it can be seen that there are three elements to consider:

- The construction firm and what it does.
- The construction environment and how it behaves.
- The boundary between the two.

This is presented in simple diagram form in Figure 1.

This book seeks to explore ways of managing the relationship between the firm and its environment and the methods which may be used to formulate a strategy which is consistent with that environment. Chapter 1 examines the changing

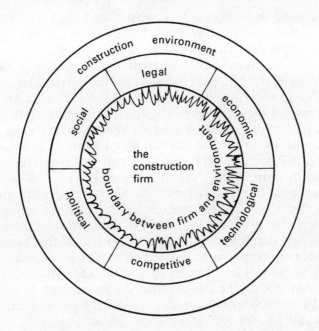

Figure 1   The construction firm in its environment

market for construction work. Although this is only one aspect of the construction market it is the element which most construction personnel can identify. The pattern and balance of workloads is appraised so that this aspect of the market can be accredited. Inevitably the usefulness of the data contained in the chapter will decay, but it is intended to provide a framework by which different markets may be analysed.

Chapter 2 looks at the nature of construction organizations. It attempts to move beyond a mere description of the industry to appraise its changing characteristics. Chapter 3 introduces readers to some strategic management concepts. It explores the nature of management decisions, be they strategic, administrative or operative in nature. These decisions may be made within a framework of two poles of strategic formulation: the formal and systematic approach and the informal and incremental approach.

Chapters 4 and 5 are more theoretical in that they seek to develop an understanding of the techniques which may be used by strategic planners in construction to envision what kind of construction environments may exist in the future. The chapters introduce methodologies for appraising future trends which will affect the construction industry. Chapter 4 considers futures and trends and Chapter 5 focuses on portfolio management, Delphi techniques and scenarios.

Chapters 1–5 therefore provide the backcloth for the formulation of strategy. Chapter 6 discusses the process of strategic management with specific reference to the construction industry. It reviews theories and research and addresses the implications for strategic management, the characteristics of the construction industry and the nature of firms in the industry.

Chapters 7 and 8 explore through case studies how strategy is made in contractors' organizations (Chapter 7) and professional consultancies (Chapter 8). As the process of strategic management is frequently directed to gaining competitive advantage the research undertaken did not seek to uncover the strategy employed but only to find out the manner in which strategy was made. Finally, Chapter 9 summarizes the main ideas from theory, practice and the case studies. It presents a contingency model of strategic management and considers the implications of such a model for construction managers and teachers and researchers in construction.

It is intended that this book will be a useful addition to the general literature on strategic management, but more importantly that it will integrate some of the concepts of strategic management with the particular management practices used within the construction industry. To quote Newcombe *et al*. (1990) 'the role of the strategic system in the survival and success of the building contracting firm cannot be overestimated'.

Part I
The Construction Environment

1

Construction in context

Strategic management of construction organizations has to take place within the context of the fortunes of the construction industry. As many researchers have documented (Hillebrandt and Cannon 1990, Shutt 1988) one of the enduring characteristics of the construction industry is its variability of demand. Taking one snapshot of the industry in 1988, in the three months January–March 1988 the orders received by contractors were 2 per cent higher than in the previous three months. The DoE recorded that in comparison with 1987 the workload of 1988 showed increases of 43 per cent for industrial work and 33 per cent for commercial orders. This was in sharp contrast to the situation of ten years earlier when output changes were equally drastic but showed declining value of orders.

This variability of demand in many ways shapes the nature of the industry and the firms which operate in it. The first point to note is that the construction industry, unlike most others, is not a single industry but is made up of several different market areas. For purposes of classification it can be divided into four areas:

- Building
- Civil engineering
- Repair and maintenance
- Materials manufacture

These may be sub-divided into separate market segments such that building is composed of housing, industrial and commercial markets. This fragmentation enables competition for work – even in boom times – to be sharp and the ease of entry into the industry and most sectors of the market stimulates this competition. Moreover the products of the construction industry tend to be fairly homogeneous in that the finished product cannot be visually identified as being the work of a particular builder (although this may not be the case with designers). This means that, in theory, there is a uniform knowledge of the market and what competitors are doing in that market. However, in practice the industry may be seen as a series of overlapping markets which define a particular service, and these markets may be divided by geography, size, type and complexity of work. Thus put bluntly there is no competition between a small repair and maintenance builder and a large national contractor; more subtly there are defined market areas for the large national contractors and whilst they may be capable of competing in all sectors of the industry the strategic choices they make confine them to one or two major market areas. Similarly the small builder may make strategic choices but more often based upon location than type of work.

So the construction industry may be broken down into several markets and this provides opportunities for constructors to focus activity or remain flexible to enable them to compete in all sectors. The question thus facing strategic planners is, what are the trends for each sector of the market?

Industrial building

The market for the industrial building sector was erratic during the period 1972–88. This volatility can be seen in the graph shown in Figure 1.1. Despite the recovery of the industrial market during the mid-1980s demand is still approximately half that of demand for commercial buildings. Several factors seem to be shaping demand. The main factor is the erosion of the manufacturing base of British industry and the change from being a country which exports manufactured goods to one which imports such goods. Inevitably this decline in the demand for goods has had a subsequent effect on the manufacturing sector's demand for industrial buildings. Also much of the industrial building work undertaken during the 1980–84 period involved the conversion of large, old factories into smaller, upgraded industrial units. The value of this work is much lower than that involved in the construction of new buildings. However, as the data from the housing

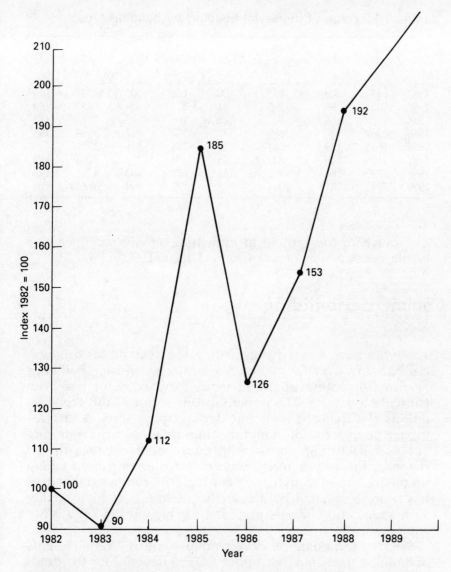

Figure 1.1 Index of value of industrial work based on 1982 prices

Source: *Housing and Construction Statistics*, HMSO

and construction statistics, published by the DoE, shown in Table 1.1 reveals there was a resurgence of industrial building in 1987 and NEDO forecasts (1992) predicted decline during 1990 followed by a modest upturn in 1992. It should be noted

Table 1.1   Value of industrial building by building type

Year	£m Factories	Index	£m Warehouses	Index	£m Other industrial	Index	£m All industrial	Index
1982	1432	100	487	100	168	100	2087	100
1983	1321	92	396	81	133	79	1850	89
1984	1687	118	495	101	160	95	2342	112
1985	2009	140	667	137	382	227	3858	185
1986	1841	129	544	112	245	146	2629	126
1987	2128	149	622	128	454	270	3204	153
1988	2359	164	806	181	778	463	4023	192
1989	2892	201	1047	214	998	594	4938	236

that much of the growth in industrial activity has been due to the construction of the Channel tunnel.

Commercial building

There has been a massive growth in the demand for commercial building over the period 1980–88. Demand for buildings by firms operating in the financial services sector has been particularly strong. The growth in this sector of the economy reflects the changed economic demography: services increasing at the expense of manufacturing; financial capital driving out manufacturing capital with consequent changes in the shape of the labour force; service sector employment taking up the job losses from manufacturing. The commercial market has been dominated by a need for buildings of high quality with space and services provided for high technology office equipment.

External technological developments and the requirements of building users have therefore shaped demand for the products of the construction industry. Demand has been particularly strong in the offices sector of the commercial market and has focused upon new building, as exemplified in the emergence of the commercial 'mega-project'. Such projects have dominated the commercial construction scene during the 1980s, comprising approximately one-third of output. The future of such mega-projects is uncertain, sensitive as they are to shifts in interest rates, political policies and continued demand for office space in the South East.

An alternative to the mega-project is the renovation and upgrading of offices built in the 1960s to meet new standards of space and comfort as well as provision for new technology. Indeed this may represent a less risky investment, although orders for large-scale projects are often broken down into phases which enable developers to spread the risk element attached to a single large project. Despite the uncertainties of the future, the sharp increase in commercial construction during the late 1980s can be seen in Figure 1.2. The property boom of the 1980s raised activity in the commercial sector from under £3000m in 1982 to a peak of £9198m in 1989. However, given the forecast for construction activity this seems set to shrink during the 1990s.

The housing market

In 1986 the market for the provision of new housing represented about 17 per cent of total construction output by value. The proportion of housing value has fallen steadily

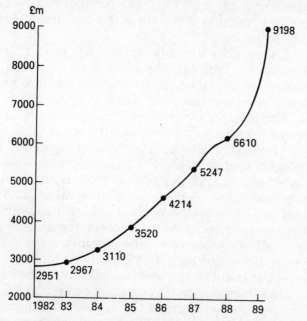

Figure 1.2 Growth of commercial construction 1982–1989

Source: NEDO (1988) *Construction Forecast 1988/89/90*

since the early 1970s when it represented some 30 per cent of the value of all new work. This is, of course, a reflection of the changing pattern of demand, with the boom in commercial building depressing the proportion of housing. However, the trend has been for the total number of housing starts to remain constant over the period 1984–88.

This trend does mask real changes in the housing market; public sector housing starts in 1989 were one-sixth of the number begun in 1974 and the projections set out in *Housing: the Government's proposals* (1987) seek to depress public sector housing investments still further. The Housing Act of 1990 will further depress the role of local authorities in the provision of housing and seek to supplement this role with private sector landlords on large housing estates and a higher profile for housing associations who can attract private funds. The necessity for housing associations to raise private funds may mean that schemes intended for single people, the elderly and single parent families will be deferred due to uncertainties about the capability of the tenants to pay an 'economic' rent. All of these facts would suggest that public sector housing provision is set to decline further. In contrast the private sector grew in 1988, the number of private sector housing starts reaching 200,000 for the first time, double the number of starts in 1980.

Table 1.2 shows the housing starts made from 1975–87 and those forecast for 1988–90. Figures 1.3 and 1.4 respectively chart the decline of public sector housing and the growth of the private sector over the same years. Why have these trends occurred? Obviously Government fiscal policies in respect of public sector spending and the restrictions on local authority capital projects have shaped the type of demand. But this would suggest that it is merely economic issues that shape the character of demand; political choices are made in respect of housing and these choices are ideological in nature.

Personal values have been changed by the political and social process so rather than the late-nineteenth-century view that 'we're all socialists now' the dominant set of cultural values of the 1980s and early 1990s has been for individualism to drive out the traditional values of collective societal responsibilities. This changed set of values can be seen as a paradigm shift which has forged preferences in models of housing provision. All these factors have a bearing on the changed pattern of the housing market and strategic planners in construction need to be aware of signals which predicate such changes.

Table 1.2 Housing starts and completions in Great Britain (thousands)

	ACTUAL												FORECAST		
	1975	1976	1977	1978	1979	1980	1981	1982	1983	1984	1985	1986	1987	1988	1989	1990
Public sector																
Starts	174	171	132	107	81	56	37	53	49	40	34	33	30	25	23	23
Completions	162	163	163	131	104	107	85	50	51	51	40	32	30	28	25	24
Private Sector																
Starts	149	155	135	157	144	99	117	141	171	157	163	176	193	200	180	175
Completions	151	152	141	149	140	128	115	125	146	157	152	171	171	185	190	175
Total																
Starts	323	326	267	264	225	155	154	194	220	197	197	209	223	225	203	198
Completions	313	315	304	280	244	235	200	175	197	208	192	203	201	213	215	199

Source: NEDO (1988) *Construction Forecasts, 1988/89/90*

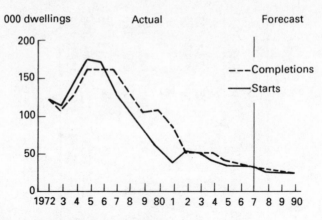

Figure 1.3   Public sector housing

Source: NEDO (1988) *Construction Forecasts 1988/89/90*

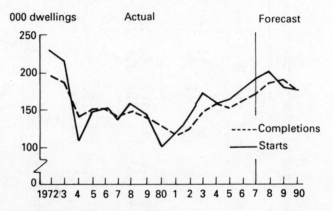

Figure 1.4   Private sector housing

Source: NEDO (1988) *Construction Forecasts 1988/89/90*

Repairs and maintenance

During the period 1972–89 overall expenditure on repair and maintenance output increased in real terms by over 30 per cent. The most pronounced increase was in the market for housing renovation although the repair and maintenance market for both public and private sector non-housing also grew strongly. This surge in repair and maintenance meant that the share of the total volume of work rose to 40 per cent and this growth is expected to continue into the 1990s. Indeed this estimate may be conservative because the official data only records work carried out by bona fide contractors; work done for cash is unlikely to be recorded and the materials used in DIY work are not included. Within the housing repair and maintenance market approximately 60 per cent of work is carried out in the private housing sector. Within the public sector local authorities are the main customers with little work being drawn from the housing associations. What factors shape expenditure in the private sector? One view is that investment in property, particularly home ownership, has been beneficial to individuals and this will have stimulated some demand. Secondly, conditions in the housing market have made it difficult and expensive for families to move and consequently existing accommodation has been upgraded. However, growth in this sector may be hampered by high interest rates and limitations of tax relief on mortgages.

Making sense of the trends

The strategic planner must assess the significance of these trends within the construction industry. It may be useful to consolidate the data to identify the major issues which are shaping demand and then explore the impact of these trends on construction firms. The first point to make is that there are two indicators that the planner can use – the value of new orders and the value of construction output. Orders are based upon contractors' returns whilst output is an aggregate of all construction work and would include estimates of the, now significant, amount of work undertaken in the frequently unrecorded repairs and maintenance sector. Therefore output is the indicator more frequently used in any data analysis.

One of the starkest trends in output is the decline in public sector work which began in the 1970s. This decline has, however, been compensated for by a growth in private sector work. Consequently changes in total output may be relatively small because changes in different sectors of the construction market have cancelled each other out. Such patterns have implications for planners in firms that specialize in particular sectors of the market. Specialized firms may suffer from a temporary shortage of work in their area and there may be barriers preventing them from transferring to more buoyant sectors of the market. These may be a lack of technical ability or the geographical distance of a project from the usual area of work. The geographical distance may deprive a firm of important local contacts with clients, designers and sub-contractors.

The geographical distribution of output is a factor worthy of consideration. Bluntly stated, the statistics show that since 1970 the regional balance of new orders in the UK (regional output data is not available) has changed with the South securing the lion's share of new orders. Thus the market for construction is now dominated by the South. Ball (1988) has calculated that if the value of new orders is taken on a per capita basis the South East generated 75 per cent more new rders than the North West during the period 1981–85. Table 1.3 shows the balance of work in the two regions from 1987 to 1989.

Table 1.3   Value of work by region, 1987–1989

Region	Value (m)
North West	9000
South East	54000

What are the implications of these trends? The decline in the public sector workload meant that firms who specialized in public sector works in the 1960s had to drastically restructure in the 1970s to be in shape for the pattern of work in the 1980s. Not only has this change had implications for the structure of firms, it has also changed the balance of staff within firms. Public sector projects are characterized by the predominance of projects which last for two years or more but many of the private sector housing projects are completed within one year. Thus contractors working on private sector housing have to bid more often and manage more projects to retain their turnover than those working on public sector projects. Ball (1988) has documented these changes by taking a snapshot of the construction industry in 1985 and examining the durations of new projects making up the new orders obtained by contractors. This is shown in Figure 1.5.

It can be seen that the larger projects tend to be a public

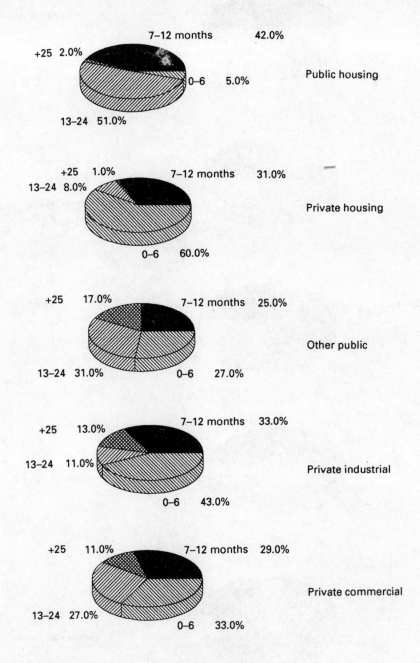

Figure 1.5 New orders in 1985 by duration of projects

Source: Ball, *Rebuilding Construction*

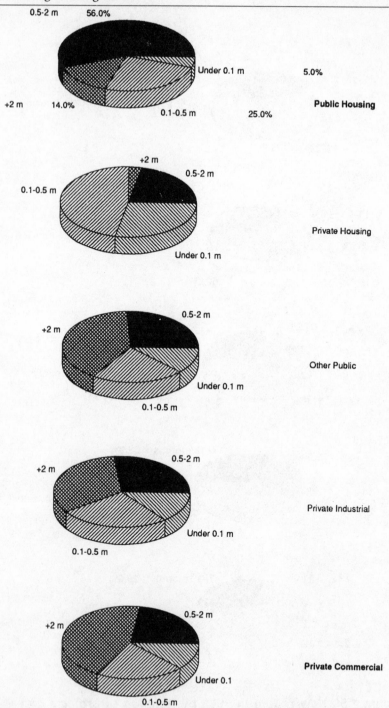

Figure 1.6 Value of new orders in 1985 displayed by size of project (data expressed as percent of total value)

Source: Ball, *Rebuilding Construction*

sector with only the large commercial projects being able to sustain projects over 25 months' duration. A similar picture emerges in respect to the value of activity (see Figure 1.6). Ball notes that 'only large office blocks and energy related ventures match the value and time scale of public sector work, and they are a quite small proportion of private sector work'.

This trend towards shorter duration projects has meant that the ratio of Administrative, Professional, Technical and Clerical staff to operatives had to increase and this has had implications for the personnel policy of firms. The change in the proportion of APTC staff as a percentage of the total workforce is shown in Figure 1.7.

A further feature of the trend towards private sector work is that much of the commercial and industrial work, as well as the housing work, is speculative. This has required land banks to be provided and has resulted in capital being tied up. Thus the maxim of highly flexible capital for building firms has had to be reappraised.

In conclusion, it is frequently difficult for firms to shape their organization to meet the changing composition of the construction markets. Large firms with specialist divisions and regional offices can manipulate resources to compete in a fashionable sector of the market, be it fashionable by type of project or services offered. Firms without a specialist division or a regional structure, however, can find it difficult to break into new market areas. The traditional medium-sized building firm, based in a depressed region, has been worst hit by changes in demand. Strategic planning could have equally

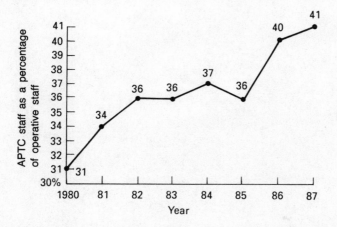

Figure 1.7   Ratio of APTC staff to operatives, 1980–1987

helped these firms to survive and service periods of market turbulence.

2

The construction organization

The construction industry is amorphous and diverse and as such it is difficult to define. There is often confusion about the extent of the industry but for the purposes of this chapter the construction industry refers to construction of all kinds, covering both building and civil engineering works. The analysis which follows will include contractors and the 'professions' (architects, quantity surveyors, engineers, etc.). Without wishing to reinforce the separation of the design aspect from the construction phase it is convenient to consider these two aspects of the industry separately.

The contractors

A simple way to outline the nature of the industry is to define it by output and by the number of firms producing this work. Indeed, the 170,000 heterogeneous and fragmented firms undertaking some £40 billion of work each year are one way of defining the industry. The workload undertaken by these firms typically includes general construction and demolition work, construction and repair of buildings, civil engineering works and installation of fixtures and fittings. This work is undertaken by a large number of small firms with a small number of large firms competing for the largest projects. This suggests that the construction industry comprises firms who differ in terms of size and scope, and even within firms there is often a great diversity of activity with different parts of the firm tackling specific sub-markets.

The very size of the construction industry makes it an

important economic entity that employs around two million people directly or indirectly in construction-related industries, constituting some 8 per cent of the total UK workforce. Equally the construction industry provides approximately 8 per cent of the Gross National Product (GNP). Construction is therefore essentially a large industry of small firms. It is staffed by operatives who are predominantly young, male and casually employed, with historically a strong craft tradition although current construction processes are replacing this tradition with a return to prefabricated components being installed by workers offering new sets of skills at the site, the craft process being transferred to off-site fabrication centres.

Despite the changes which have taken place in the construction production process, the tradition of design as a separate entity from production remains. This separation has important ramifications for the classification of the construction industry: design, quite properly, can be seen as a service industry but is construction better defined as 'manufacturing'? Given the nature and diversity of activities carried out in the construction industry, there is a natural tendency for the industry to be viewed as manufacturing in nature rather than a service industry. Newcombe (1976) submitted that 'it is a misnomer to classify the construction industry as a service industry along with banking, insurance and retailing'. The definition of construction is important as the way in which one looks at the industry defines its markets, and consequently, the strategic processes which are used to govern and direct the construction organization. Newcombe's analysis suggests that the principal functions performed in the manufacturing industries can be mirrored in the construction industry although he uses different titles for various functions. He claims that the functions carried out in construction are comparable to those of manufacture as illustrated in Table 2.1.

This view is not orthodox. Fleming (1980) relates the classification of the industry to the production processes used in construction and manufacture:

> the relative and absolute cost advantages which often favour large scale operations and large established firms in manufacturing are of little importance . . . as factors encouraging the growth of greater industrial concentration in construction. . . . The site based nature of construction where each site is necessarily a temporary place of work, and the individuality of most projects ensures that the conditions necessary for the existence of many

**Table 2.1 Principal functions performed in the manufacturing
and construction industries**

Manufacturing	Construction	Principle of Function
Marketing	Estimating	Identification/creation of markets, and selling of end 'products'
Production	Construction	Organization, movement and assembling of various materials, components, etc.
Purchasing	Buying	Acquisition, bulk or otherwise of production materials and components for a project or in-lieu of a project

Source: Newcombe (1976)

technical scale economies, mainly centralization of production of
standard products using specialized production techniques do
not apply.

This view is supported by Hillebrandt (1974) who considers
construction to be a service industry. This conclusion is drawn
from the evidence of what builders actually do. She notes
that 'construction may be regarded as one industry whose
total product is durable buildings and works'. It is 'the contracting part of the industry which undertakes to organize,
move and assemble various materials and component parts
so that they form a composite whole of a building or other
work. The product which the contracting industry is providing is basically the service of moving earth and material, of
assembling and managing the whole business'. This observation recognizes the changes that have been taking place in
the construction industry over the last twenty years, resulting
in a strong differentiation between contractors who provide
management services and contractors who undertake to build
the physical product.

The separation of the industry into these two distinct areas
has been one industrial response to the relatively high levels
of risk which are perceived to exist within the market. This
risk is being passed down the line to those who actually do
the construction work. The separation of the management
and the doing is reflected in the technical processes involved
in each aspect of construction work and, therefore, industrial

classification may be based upon differences in the technical processes undertaken. Large firms providing management contracting and project management services may be regarded as part of the service industry, whereas those providing resources which are used to construct the building might be better described as manufacturing style organizations.

A further complication exists when large organizations are highly diverse in their activities. Those firms designated as building and civil engineering contractors offer quite distinct services which operate in distinct markets and their staff may not be generally interchangeable. Large construction organizations may be involved in building houses for sale which again forms a different market and requires different sets of resources and management skills. Many contractors have moved into property investment as a means of vertical integration, as a mechanism for forward integration. They have also sought to move backwards into product manufacture in order to stabilize the environment in which they work. Contractors are therefore seeking to spread risks by strategies of related diversification into connected markets. Catherwood (1966) distils this approach rather succinctly when observing that 'a successful general contractor may fail miserably in speculative house building . . . or in civil engineering, conversely a civil engineering contractor may undertake a building contract at his peril'.

In the light of the above observations the construction industry may be defined in terms of several distinct construction markets some of which provide a service, others which reveal characteristics of a manufacturing organization. A typical classification divides these into five business arenas, principally: civil engineering, building, property development, estate development (housing) and construction product manufacture. Larger companies will operate in all sectors. Their strategy is to diversify activities from relatively specialized bases, for example, a base centred on a product or service offered, or, more frequently, defined by the geographical area in which the company operates. As firms seek to grow the most common diversification has followed the trend towards backward integration into the production of construction materials and forward integration into property development. This trend is coupled with diversification outside the UK by companies setting up overseas operations in former Empire territories and moves to the Middle East and other developing areas as work has become available. However, such foreign adventures tend to reflect a poverty of domestic opportunities and the strength of overseas governments' ability to pay for infrastructure development. Middle Eastern states, rich in oil dollars, have become difficult markets for UK contractors who have been faced with stern competition from China and Korea.

The balance of overseas construction activity to domestic markets can be seen in Table 2.2. Whilst these figures suggest stability they mask the highly turbulent state of overseas markets. For example, in 1977 the value of contracts obtained in the Middle East was £862m. By 1987 this had declined to £125m. In the same period workload in Africa had halved. These traditional overseas markets have been replaced by massive expansions in the Americas (1977 – £159m.; 1987 – £990m.) and the EEC (1977 – £16m.; 1987 – £213m.). Not only is the UK construction industry dependent on overseas work for about 10 per cent of its output, but also foreign firms are increasingly looking to the UK market. Foreign companies have seized opportunities presented by the manpower shortages of the late 1980s and the UK has imported materials and expertise from many parts of the world. Japanese and American contractors and project managers have been particularly predatory in the field of commercial development.

All the facts suggest that the contracting part of the

Table 2.2 The balance between domestic and overseas orders (1985 prices)

	Domestic £	Overseas £	% of overseas work
1977	14643	1597	10.9
1978	15372	1388	9.0
1979	13957	1261	9.0
1980	11507	1024	8.9
1981	12451	1516	12.2
1982	13166	2350	17.8
1983	15192	2242	14.7
1984	15788	2527	16.0
1985	15343	1491	9.0
1986	16593	1884	11.3
1987	19759	3155	15.9

Source: DoE Housing and Construction Statistics

construction industry may be described as a highly competitive industry which offers services and manufacturing type activities to clients in an international market. However, the picture may be very different for the 'professions' within the industry.

Yes

The professions

In common with contractors the professions associated with the construction industry may be seen as 'generalists', in that in order to develop and retain flexibility in the face of changing market and economic hazards, they tend to adopt a generalist attitude to their work. Thus architects tend not to specialize in one particular building type or method of construction. This means that most firms are prepared to tackle most, though not necessarily all, building problems within their particular resources. The strategic choices which the professions need to make are therefore related to their markets and most, like contractors, have chosen flexibility as a mechanism for survival and growth.

This concept of the professions as generalists relates to the product – the building being built – rather than to the service being provided to clients. The professions rely on gradations of specialisms with structural or services engineers providing specialist design facilities and quantity surveyors providing expertise in financial management of projects. These are the traditional professions but professions related to the control of particular aspects of the construction process are also involved. For example, professional project management firms who are independent of the contractors and sub-contractors actually executing the work provide specialist management for clients. More recently firms involved in programming the whole of the construction process, from inception to completion, have come into being. This development resulted from the identification of a gap in the market: architects (or other designers) control quality, quantity surveyors control costs but there was no specialist to control 'time'. As professional boundaries change new opportunities emerge and contract claims specialists, quality control experts, building envelope engineers (engineers who are commissioned to design cladding systems for the outsides of buildings) and other professionals currently on the margins of the construction process are redrawing the contours of the responsibilities of the professionals. A strategic consequence of this is the potential for discovering and exploiting new areas in the market.

The designers (architects and engineers)

It is not appropriate here to describe the traditional role of designers; this section merely seeks to identify the structure of the professions. The organization of a design practice will have implications for the strategy of the organization. Table 2.3 provides an overview of the design professions and reveals that a large proportion of designers in private architectural practice are based in one-person or small practices.

Whilst the work undertaken by private practices varies with the size and turnover of the practice certain generalizations may be made:

1. The smaller practices deal mainly with private individual clients or with larger clients requiring small-scale works;
2. The larger practices are able to deal with corporate clients whether the work is public or private in nature. Commercial and industrial projects feature heavily in the portfolio of buildings designed and major feasibility studies frequently appear in the portfolios of many larger practices.

Important changes have taken place to the strategic role of the architect in the construction process during the 1980s. Perceptions of the architect's role may have resulted in changes which have emphasized the design aspect and diminished the project management role. Certainly new procurement methods such as management contracting and construction management, project management and even design and build methods have imposed changes on the way architects organize their practices. Clients are more often seeking 'one stop shopping' for the purchase of their construction services and so architects have combined, formally or informally, to provide multi-discipline practices which encompass the full range of expertise necessary for the erection of a building.

The changes in the way buildings are procured have taken place against a backcloth of greater commercial awareness amongst architectural practices. The code of conduct for the architectural profession has been changed to allow architects to advertise their services and, more importantly, to become directors of companies connected with construction, property or development. As architects move away from their position

Table 2.3 Full-time mainly architectural practices and numbers employed by size of practice, 1980, UK

Practice size (No. of architectural staff)	Practices	Principals		Employees				Total	
	Number	No.	Av. per practice	Architects		Other staff		No.	% of total
				No.	Av. per practice	No.	Av. per practice		
1–2	2 216	2 604	1.2	181	0.1	438	0.2	3 223	11.5
3–5	1 189	2 106	1.8	818	0.7	1 976	1.7	4 900	17.5
6–10	629	1 529	2.4	1 099	1.7	2 429	3.9	5 057	18.0
11–30	434	1 992	4.6	2 353	5.4	3 948	9.1	8 293	29.6
31–50	72	574	8.0	1 097	15.2	1 490	20.7	3 161	11.3
51 and over	35	553	15.8	1 293	36.9	1 538	43.9	3 384	12.1
Total	4 574	9 358	2.0	6 841	1.5	11 819	2.6	28 018	100

Source: Reproduced from RIBA Statistics Section, *Census of Private Architectural Practices 1980* (RIBA, 1981) Tables 1 and 7

as 'an occupation possessing a skilled intellectual technique' (Kaye, 1960) set within the framework of a voluntary association (RIBA) with its code of conduct, they are offered a new range of strategic choices. Modern architectural practices tend to corporate identities and require strategic planning to ensure their survival and growth.

Civil, structural and services engineers are in a similar position to architects. However, the professional associations for engineers are not as involved with professional firms as are RIBA or RICS. The principal vehicle for policing consulting engineers' conduct is the Association of Consulting Engineers (ACE) which lays down broad guidelines for conduct and fees, etc. Whilst the engineering professions have not experienced the plethora of changes which have shaped the architects' role they have to operate in the same construction environment. Therefore engineering consultancies have sought to combine with others to enable them to survive and grow.

One of the most potent arenas for strategic choice has been in the price charged for services supplied. In most industries such decisions would be part of the pricing policy and this would be set following an appraisal of the market for the product. Yet it is only since 1982 that architects and engineers have been able to compete on the basis of fees paid for their work. (Fee competition for quantity surveyors followed in 1983.) The abolition of the fee scales set by RIBA and ACE opened up the market to competition from other consultants but also provided opportunities for practices to take the lead on price as well as on the services offered to clients. The release from fee scales came only after several hostile reports, including the 1967 Prices and Incomes Board report on architects' fees and the 1973 referral of architects' fees to the Monopolies Commission. The Monopolies and Mergers Commission Report (1977) recommended that uniform fees be abandoned and that architects be allowed to compete on fees. A similar conclusion was promulgated for surveyors.

This redirection of the professions into business entities has meant that several partnerships have become public limited companies and some have sought listings on the Unlisted Securities Markets and the largest firms have achieved a full stock exchange listing. These events presage a new interest in corporate planning by the construction consultant who will look to take stock of business opportunities within the construction environment.

Part II
The Theory of Strategy

3

Concepts of strategic management

The aim of this chapter is to consider some of the more important ideas presented in strategic management literature. The major themes of the chapter are: the concepts of strategy, the introduction of a simple model of a firm, the environment within which the firm operates and the strategic management process that evolves from it. The role of the strategist is discussed together with the options that are available to strategic decision-makers. Finally, a typology of strategic behaviours is introduced.

The concept of strategy and the nature of strategic decisions

There are common themes in the definition of strategy. Strategy is concerned with the *means* to meet *ends*, that is it is concerned with achieving *objectives*. A strategy is also a set of rules for guiding decisions about organizational behaviour. Strategies may be explicit or implicit, kept within the confines of the senior management team or pervading the organization to produce a sense of common direction. Two views have emerged on the nature of strategy. The first perspective views strategy as a *planning* mode. A strategy is worked out in advance, is explicit and managers develop a systematic and structured plan to meet objectives. The second perspective sees strategy as an *evolutionary* mode. From this viewpoint strategy evolves over time, is not thought out and planned but is a stream of significant decisions. Each perspective has different implications for the strategic management process.

The evolutionary mode, or logical incrementalism in Ansoff's (1987) terms, is not concerned with the future validity of the firm's basic direction but is only concerned with the contribution that new proposals can make to growth and profitability. It has been suggested that a comprehensive, systematic approach to strategic planning (the planning mode) can challenge and reformulate the strategic logic of the firm's future development. Strategic management literature differentiates between first and second generation strategic planning. In first generation planning strategists will only look at one set of alternatives whereas in second generation or contingency planning multiple sets of alternatives will be considered perhaps with a series of strategies worked out to allow for anticipated changes in the environment. First generation planning leads to a *programmed strategy* where the strategy is worked out in such detail that it becomes difficult to alter once implemented. A *contingency strategy*, on the other hand, requires the strategist to choose the best strategy under a given set of circumstances but to have the flexibility inherent within it to be able to adapt to changing environmental circumstances. This requires careful environmental scanning, monitoring and evaluation. Second generation planning leads to contingency strategy formation where 'what if' situations are created for decision-makers.

The nature of decisions facing the firm can be broken down into three areas:

- Operational decisions, dealing with the transforming of inputs into outputs. The bulk of a firm's time will be devoted to such activities.
- Administrative decisions, concerned with organizational structuring and resource allocation.
- Strategic decisions which relate the firm to its business environment. Their effect is diffused throughout the organization over time and therefore has an impact on the previous two forms of decisions. This book is primarily concerned with this type of decision-making.

The following section develops a simple diagnostic model for analysing a firm in the context of managers operating as decision-makers within an 'organization'.

A diagnostic model of a firm

The term 'firm' is used here to represent an entity that is a social organization and has as one of its objectives the aim of making a profit. For analytical purposes firms can be viewed in general as having some form of vertical structure, or hierarchy, and operating within an environment (see Figure 3.1). The external environment of a firm can be viewed as an envelope which surrounds the firm and has an impact on it through different types of pressure. The firm is delineated from the external environment by a boundary. The firm as an economic entity is also a social system and its boundary is moveable or permeable because people from within it are in constant interaction with others from organizations outside the boundary, either by telephone or through meetings, etc. A particular firm has, therefore, spheres of influence that go beyond the buildings, production plants or facilities that it occupies. Inputs from the environment will cross the firm's boundary and are transformed through the production process into outputs. By way of example, in the case of a construction company its environment would comprise government departments, competitors, suppliers, sub-contractors, consultants. The spheres of influence of a quantity surveying consultancy could perhaps be best explored by taking the case of a negotiation of a contractual claim. In this instance the

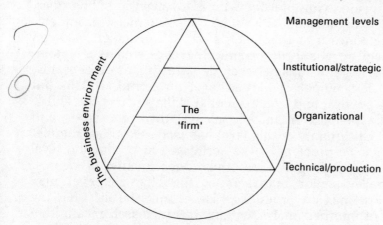

Figure 3.1 A simple model of a firm

consultant quantity surveyor, as a representative of his or her firm, may visit a contractor's head office or perhaps a site. The consultant's organizational boundary has been extended to within the contractor's office. For an architectural practice, the production process is, in part, concerned with the transformation of ideas and information from the client into outputs in the form of a set of drawings for the contractor.

In considering the hierarchy of a firm, Figure 3.1 identifies different levels of management. The *institutional* or *strategic level* is concerned with adapting the organization to the external environment; at the *organizational level* the primary focus of managers is one of the integration of lateral and vertical relationships; finally, the *technical* or *production level* is concerned with transforming inputs from the environment into outputs which can subsequently be sold in the market place. Each level within the firm has different properties in terms of the level of uncertainty encountered and also requires different skills of managers.

The production level is task oriented, uncertainty is relatively low and routines can be developed for handling repetitive tasks. The production level is concerned very much with the present and getting the job done. It requires of managers, therefore, a task orientation, technical skills and a short-term time horizon. This would correspond to the site agent level in a construction company, draughtsman level in an architectural or engineering consultancy or an assistant surveyor in a quantity surveying practice who is involved in billing operations. The organizational level has a requirement for integration. The concern at this level is one of mediation between the strategic level and the technical level as well as maintaining lateral relationships between departments or other teams. There is less emphasis at this level on technical skills but more on political and organizational skills such as the ability to handle people, organizational systems, procedures and controls. Uncertainty at this level has increased. For example, there could be problems to be addressed at production level or between colleagues in other departments or teams. Additionally, senior managers at the strategic level may require briefings on production issues and the fact that the number of interpersonal situations has increased means that managers are facing a more dynamic situation. Mintzberg (1973) has indicated that managers can spend up to 70 per cent of their time in interpersonal exchanges. Typical examples at the organizational level in the construction industry would be contracts managers in contracting companies or team leaders in consultancy organizations. Managers at this level need to operate in two different time frames, the short term when dealing with the production level and the longer term when dealing with the strategic level. At the strategic level managers are concerned with those issues that relate the firm to the environment. The question here is one of survival and adaptation to the pressures of the external environment. Uncertainty is at its highest and information is less, is ambiguous and unstructured. Managers are concerned with the longer term and there is a requirement for conceptual and judgemental skills and the ability to handle, analyse and reformulate unstructured information received from the environment and internally from within the firm. Typical examples in construction would be director level in a contractors and partner level in consultancies. The development of skills and concern with the firm's requirements at this level have tended to be neglected in the construction industry.

In summary, this section has presented a simple model of a firm with different layers of managers requiring different skills and time horizons, and making different types of decisions. The firm operates in an environment to which it has to adapt. The following sections take up the issues surrounding analysis at the strategic level of a firm and elaborate on the model outlined above.

The environment

Firms operate within an industry environment and the construction industry environment has been described in Chapter 2. There are five major forces determining industry structure and these jointly establish the profit potential in an industry. An awareness of their joint influences is important for understanding the competitive environment facing the individual firm. Figure 3.2 sets out these forces diagrammatically. Described briefly, *buyers* and *suppliers* have similar effects in that if they are powerful, profit margins can be pushed down. Buyers (or clients) as a group are particularly important in construction since their advisers, in the form of the construction professions, can dictate the rules of competition for contractors, especially through the choice of procurement path. In the case of suppliers, construction is a highly interconnected

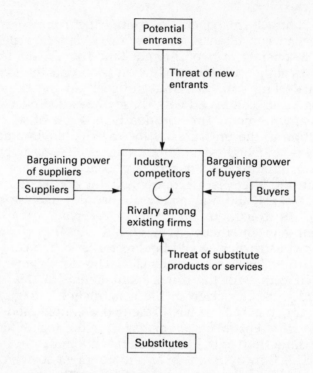

Figure 3.2   Porter's industry structure framework

Source: Porter, *Competitive Strategy* (1980)

industry through materials inputs from other industries. Therefore, where industrial concentration in other industries may be high the opportunity for suppliers to influence input costs could be considerable. *Threat of entry* is concerned with the likelihood of new competitors entering the industry. This is dependent on the presence or absence of entry barriers. It is often claimed that entry and exit barriers to the construction industry are low. However, others have suggested that there are subtle forms of entry barriers present in construction that have no direct counterpart in manufacturing. This stems directly from the heterogeneity and characteristics of the industry and the nature of the markets within it (see also Chapter 2). *Threat of substitute products* or services is not an easy concept to apply in the construction industry. For example, Chapter 2 has suggested that the product in construction is a mix of services or manufacturing depending on the point of view adopted. The critical issue in deciding what is or is not a substitute, according to Porter (1980), is that the substitute must undertake the same function. In construction there are similarities between design and build and certain types of project management, for example, executive project management. The function served is to provide a service to the client with single point responsibility to integrate and control the relationship between design and construction. Other examples of possible substitutes include construction management and management contracting and refurbishment versus new build options. Finally, the *extent of competitive rivalry* is determined by the degree of mutual dependency or interaction between competitors and the likelihood of this setting off retaliatory strategic moves between them.

Other factors operate in the external environment in addition to the above and include:

- Socio-economic trends
- Technological changes
- Demographic shifts
- Government influences other than through the economy
- Industry associations and interest groups
- Communities

The following section moves from the external environment of the firm inside its boundary and considers the role of decision-making, the nature of the strategic management process and the role of the strategist.

The firm and the strategic management process

The strategic management process
The strategic management process is the manner in which strategic decision-makers determine objectives and make choices to achieve those objectives within the context of the resources available and the firm's mission. The strategic management process has three interlocking parts: strategy formulation, strategy implementation and strategy feedback. Strategy formulation is concerned with matching the firm's capabilities with its environment. In terms of the model outlined in Figure 3.1, strategy formulation is undertaken at the strategic level, is implemented throughout the organization and the results are monitored and fed back to the strategic level for appropriate action.

Strategic formulation

The strategic formulation process commences with the mission of the firm – its long-term goal. This requires a series of objectives to be set and met with strategies as the means of attaining these objectives. The strategic formulation process requires an assessment of the strengths and weaknesses of the firm (the internal diagnosis) and the opportunities and threats in the environment (the external diagnosis). This assessment is usually termed the SWOT analysis.

The strategic formulation process is affected by a number of factors:

- Environmental forces and pressures outlined above.
- Resources available to the organization.
- Internal power relationships within the firm. Organizational politics have an important impact on strategy formulation as established power groupings or coalitions may be threatened.

- Strategists' value systems. A person's values are affected by education, family background, attitudes and experiences.
- Organizations may lack information about their environments or may not have the requisite skills to undertake strategy formulation and subsequently implementation.
- The firm's history and its relationship to perceptions of the current situation.

Mission, objectives and strategy

The firm's mission is its *raison d'être*, that is, the fundamental reason for the firm's existence and what it wants to become over time. A mission may be narrowly or broadly defined and will probably have emanated from the founding entrepreneur's vision of what the firm should become. However, as businesses develop, change and diversify there should be a common thread linking the various parts of a business. The firm's mission may be encapsulated within a mission statement and will be probably in qualitative terms.

The mission should be clearly articulated and allow action to be taken based on it (Jauch and Glueck 1988). The mission statement should be:

- Precise
- Indicate how the objectives are to be accomplished
- Indicate the major components of strategy.

A firm's objectives stem from the mission or mission state-ment and will be expressed normally in quantifiable terms. Objectives perform four important functions:

- They facilitate comparison of actual versus projected per-formance and indicate the extent of the strategic gap.
- They can be prioritized. High order objectives can allow the coordination and integration of lower level objectives within the firm.
- They can have a time horizon associated with them which can provide a mechanism for appraising the firm and its managers. If this is to be undertaken then objectives must be specific and verifiable.
- They create a product market focus for the strategy.

A firm's strategy can have four distinct components:

- *Business scope.* The business definition in terms of cus-tomers served, customer needs and how these are being met.
- *Resource utilization* to match distinctive competencies. This means resourcing properly the areas in which the firm has well developed technical skills or knowledge bases.
- Isolating areas of *competitive advantage*, that is, superiority over competitors. It has been suggested that this will be located in the technical core of a business.
- Areas of business *synergy*. Where business areas interact so that the effect of the whole is greater than the sum of the parts.

Strategic choice
Strategic choice refers to the fact that strategists have a range of options available to them. Underlying the notion of stra-tegic choice is that:

- Strategic decision-makers have a degree of latitude in making choices and are not bound purely by environmen-tal, technological or other forces.
- Firms have the power to influence their environments as well as be influenced by them.
- Managerial perceptions and evaluations act as a mediating variable between the environment and the actions taken by the organization.

Whilst the concept of strategic choice has been criticized it has important analytical implications in highlighting those variables over which management are able to exercise some control (or can influence in their favour) in comparison to the constraints that have to be considered in determining the latitude available to the decision-maker. Following on from this, strategic choice involves, therefore, the selection amongst a number of options of the strategic alternative(s) that best meet the firm's objectives. The choice will be made using a set of criteria to guide decision-makers. It has been suggested that the eventual decision should be based on the criteria of *suitability* – the degree of fit between the proposed strategy and the situation identified in the SWOT analysis; *feasibility* – the practicalities of the strategy to be adopted; and *acceptability* – once chosen, is the strategy acceptable.

There are a number of approaches or techniques available to the strategist to assist in the decision-making process. These are product portfolio analysis, lifecycle analysis, competitive advantage analysis and synergy. Chapter 4 deals with the issues surrounding portfolio analysis and introduces, in the context of the construction industry, the idea of project portfolio analysis. Having identified the best strategy for achieving the firm's objectives, the next stages of the strategic management process are implementation and feedback.

Strategic implementation and feedback

Strategic implementation and feedback occur through 'organization'. A firm as an 'organization' is a social entity in its own right but also forms part of the wider social system. People bring to the work setting their beliefs, values, prejudices and biases. Therefore, implementation by the organization requires coordination of activities through some form of structure. Thus strategy implementation requires three basic questions to be answered:

1. Who has the responsibility for carrying out the strategies?
2. What must be done in order for implementation to be successful?
3. How will the implementation process work?

This requires the planning of resources through some kind of budgetary framework, the designing and staffing of an appropriate organizational structure and ensuring that the proper systems and controls are in place to enable the behaviour of individuals to be directed towards achieving strategic objectives. The implementation process is the area most often neglected in the strategic management process.

Feedback, allowing any corrective action to be taken, will be provided to the strategic level by measuring actual performance via the systems and procedures that have been set up against the quantitative criteria established for strategic objectives. The next section deals with the role of the strategist in the strategic management process.

The role of the strategist

The primary role of the strategist is to:

- Monitor, analyse and diagnose the environment in order to anticipate opportunities and threats.
- Assess the degree of risk associated with any opportunities in the environment.
- Assess the firm's strengths and weaknesses.
- Match the opportunities present in the environment with the firm's strengths whilst minimizing the weaknesses against possible threats.
- Develop strategies, decide amongst alternatives and allocate resources to enable selected strategies to be undertaken.
- Monitor results and take corrective action via feedback.

Depending on the size of the firm, the strategist may be an individual or a team. As firm size increases considerably it will be the Managing Director acting in conjunction with the Board of Directors.

The environmental diagnosis undertaken by the strategist as part of the formulation process can be affected by a number of factors. These include psychological mood, a person's cognitive structure in terms of attitudes to risk and underlying experience, attitude towards change and whether a proactive versus reactive stance is adopted by an individual. Where the diagnosis and formulation process is undertaken by a team 'groupthink' may be present. Underlying the idea of groupthink is the notion that group dynamics change perceptions subtly and increase the tendency towards taking riskier decisions than, for example, any one of the group would take as an individual if away from the collective decision situation. In a team or group situation it is advisable to appoint a 'devil's advocate' who will challenge or question group decisions in order to counteract the possibility of groupthink.

Strategic alternatives

Depending on the analysis of the firm's strengths and weaknesses and the environmental opportunities and threats (the results of the SWOT analysis) the firm's strategists face a number of strategic options or alternatives on which to compete. The basis of competition is the three generic strategies identified by Porter (1980), namely:

- *Cost leadership*: where attention is directed to the cost structure of the firm and careful attention is paid, therefore, to controlling cost.
- *Differentiation*: where the firm attempts to create the perception that it is different or unique from its competitors. Whilst the firm's cost structure cannot be ignored this is not the primary weapon of competition.
- *Focus*: where the firm's attention is focused on a buyer group, a particular product line or geographic market. This is a niche strategy whereby the firm carves out a competitive arena which may be a sub-set of a broader market.

Since the latter strategy can also employ cost leadership or differentiation, it has been argued that there are, in practice, only two major generic strategies: cost or differentiation. There are risks associated with each of the generic strategies and individual strategies require different sets of resources and skills for their implementation.

There are a number of directions that strategists can take:

- To opt for operational changes only whilst environmental changes of which the firm is unaware are underway.
- To consolidate or stabilize. This is a positive decision to remain within existing markets but to make changes in the way the firm operates and also track changes in the environment.
- To retrench. This may be the least frequently used strategy and is sometimes one that may be overlooked for strategic repositioning and/or redefining the business. It is a difficult option for managers to pursue as divestment may imply failure whereas expansion strategies may be perceived as recipes for managerial success.
- To penetrate existing markets; to develop new products and maintain existing markets; to develop new markets whilst maintaining present products.
- To diversify. There are two forms of diversification,

related or unrelated. The former, also called concentric diversification, occurs within the broad confines of the industry within which a firm operates. Related diversification within the construction industry can be extensive in that it can include, for example, building and civil engineering contracting, the production of building materials, plant hire firms, onshore construction of oil-rig platforms and property development. These can all be perceived as related to aspects of the construction industry or to construction activity. Unrelated diversification, also called conglomerate diversification, takes the firm outside the industry, markets or products within which it presently operates. Trafalgar House and P. & O. are examples of conglomerates with interests in construction, who have followed a strategy of unrelated diversification.

There are three means of achieving strategic development:

- Internally where the firm invests its own capital to set up and operate a new venture. This option is often the primary vehicle of growth.
- Externally through acquisition or merger. This option is often used where speed is of the essence or when a market is growing very slowly or is stagnant. The biggest problem with acquisition is the integration of the acquired with the acquiring firm or in the case of merger the successful integration of two organizational cultures to produce a new culture that represents something other than the dominance of one culture over another.
- A combination strategy which combines elements of internal and external development through contractual agreements. An example of such a strategy in the construction industry is the use of joint ventures.

Finally, there are two additional approaches associated with diversification which can be linked with internal or external strategic development. The first of these is integration, either forward or backward, to increase the value added. In these instances the firm, usually through acquisition, moves, in the case of forward integration, towards the eventual end purchaser of goods or services. In the case of backward integration the firm moves towards raw materials supply. In a construction firm forward integration would be in the direction of property development and backward integration would be into building materials production. The second approach is internationalization, in which the firm expands its geographic operating boundaries and moves from operating in a purely domestic business environment to operating in an international one. Chapter 4 will discuss the implications for the construction industry of these two approaches in more detail.

Strategic behaviour

As firms analyse and respond to the environment through strategy formulation, implementation and feedback, it is possible to discern a series of strategic behaviours. A number of different typologies of organizations and their behaviour have been formulated. The typologies that are most useful for describing the strategic behaviour of the variety of organizations in the construction industry and the implications that stem from them for practice are those of Mintzberg (1979), Miles and Snow (1978) and Ansoff (1987).

Mintzberg's typology

Mintzberg has identified five ideal structural types.

Simple structure

This has direct supervision as its prime coordinating mechanism. The key part of the firm is at the strategic level and as its name implies the structure is simple and is uncluttered by rules and regulations. There is little, if any, in the way of functional departments and there is little planning or training but there is considerable personal interaction. The organizational structure can be described as organic. This type of structure characterizes small organizations. A small sub-contracting firm, employing a few operatives would be an example in the construction industry. A one or two person architectural, quantity surveying or engineering consultancy would also typify this structure.

Machine bureaucracy

Standardization of work processes is the prime coordinating mechanism of this structure. This type of structure characterizes large firms in stable environments which use highly routine technology. There are many rules and regulations, functional departments and centralized decision-making that follows the chain of command. There is a sharp distinction between line and staff and a well-developed administrative structure. A building component manufacturer would typically have this structure.

Professional bureaucracy

This structure has as its prime coordinating mechanism the standardization of skills. The operating core or production level is the key part of the firm. This type of firm is staffed by specialists – professionals – with highly-developed knowledge and skills who have considerable work autonomy. Decision-making is, therefore, decentralized. The difference between this and the former type of bureaucracy is that the machine type has standardization developed within the organization. Standardization with the professional type occurs outside the organization through educational and professional institutions. A typical example in the construction industry would be a large engineering, quantity surveying or architectural practice, especially one that has diversified internationally. Some of the quantity surveying practices studied by Male (1984) and architectural practices by Hillier (1979) would typify this structure.

Ad hocracy

The prime coordinating mechanism of this structure is mutual adjustment through interpersonal interaction. Mintzberg differentiates between the administrative and operative ad hocracy depending on the nature of the skills brought to the task. However, there may be interaction between the two forms. Ad hocracies are team based and temporary in nature. They are staffed typically by professionals with a high level of expertise, and flexibility for adaptation and problem-solving with minimal supervision. Decision-making is decentralized with democratic decision-making common. Influence in an ad hocracy is through professional expertise rather than positional authority. The ad hocracy is typified by the project structure in construction.

Divisional structure

This structure has as its prime coordinating mechanism the standardization of outputs. The divisional structure creates a series of relatively autonomous smaller firms with functional structures. Groupings tend to be by markets served and the strategic business unit concept (SBU) is applied to each of the

relatively autonomous operating units. The divisional structure is common in the construction industry especially among
the larger contractors. Portfolio analysis, which will be discussed in Chapter 5, is a particularly pertinent technique to
apply to this structure.

Miles and Snow's typology

The typology developed by Miles and Snow reflects the
relationship between managers' perceptions of the environment, the internal power and political structure of a firm and
the relationship between strategy, structure and process. This
typology has been used by Usdiken (1987) in a study of the
Turkish construction industry. Miles and Snow have identified four types:

Defenders

They are concerned with stability and efficiency. They will
concentrate on a narrow range of products or services and
opt for a niche strategy through market penetration. There is
an emphasis on hierarchical control, with centralized decision-
making, limited environmental scanning but intensive planning for cost efficiency. Defenders opt for a focus strategy on
the basis of cost leadership.

Prospectors

They opt for flexibility and the exploitation of new market
and product opportunities offered by the environment. There
is a stress therefore on environmental scanning. The structure
is flexible, stressing informality, with few routines and procedures and it will be decentralized. The prospector in its search
for new opportunities is, however, likely to be effective but
inefficient.

Analysers

The analyser attempts to combine aspects of the defender and
the prospector, seeking to minimize risk while attempting to
maximize the opportunity for profit. Analysers move into new
markets or products only after market viability is proven. This
type of firm is likely to adopt a strategy of imitation. The
structure of the analyser will reflect the dual nature of its
operations. Parts of the organization will have high levels of
standardization with the presence of routines and procedures.
Other parts of the organization will be adaptive and have the
characteristics of the prospector.

Reactors

This type of firm is caught between the other three types and represents an organization with inconsistent and unstable strategic behaviour patterns which attempts, unsuccessfully, to pursue one of the other three strategies. Reactors respond, therefore, inappropriately to the environment, have a poor performance and do not pursue a particular strategy in an aggressive manner.

Ansoff's typology

The final typology to be discussed is that of Ansoff (1987). Ansoff identifies three modes of managed strategic behaviour:

Proactive systematic mode

Where change in the environment is incremental the firm will use extrapolation of historical trends and performance. This typifies long-range planning as opposed to a strategic management approach. Where environmental change is discontinuous and therefore more difficult to predict, there would be a periodic and systematic assessment of the firm's future direction. Thus, the firm would be adopting a strategic management approach. Strategic thinking and decision-making is explicit.

Proactive ad hoc mode

In this mode there is no centrally guided approach to strategic development; the emphasis is on incrementalism. Environmental scanning and search will take place but not in a planned way. Where change in the environment is incremental 'bottom up' procedures would be used from the lower levels of the firm. Initiatives would be periodic, and incremental, that is, based very much on current directions with the emphasis on research and development and/or marketing. Where changes in the environment are basically incremental but periods of discontinuity occur the firm will use a trial and error approach in relation to perceived changes in the environment and focus on what are seen as important issues. Strategic thinking and decision-making is implicit.

Reactive mode

This mode has similarities with the reactor type of firm identified by Miles and Snow. The emphasis is on minimization of strategic changes. Any changes in performance that have been identified by management will be considered to be operative as opposed to strategic. Where changes in the environment are incremental the firm will rely on trial and error approaches triggered by indicators of poor performance. Where change in the environment is discontinuous the firm will search for a panic solution when confronted with a crisis.

In summary, strategic management literature has identified a number of different typologies that can be used to describe firms. The implications of these for the construction industry will be developed further in Chapter 9, p. 140. The following section deals with two final important topics in strategic management, the experience curve and the product life cycle.

Other strategic management concepts

The experience curve

The concept of the experience curve stems from the work of the Boston Consulting Group. It has its critics. The underlying assumption behind the curve is that price levels will be similar for similar products in the same market segment. Products are therefore close substitutes. The difference in the level of profits between companies is therefore dependent on the costs of an individual firm. Thus over time as the total number of units produced increases the unit cost will decrease. The reasoning behind this is related to the fact that people will learn to do a job more effectively over time; that through increasing specialization and economies of scale, capital costs decrease relative to increasing capacity; and that gaining and holding market share is important because of the postulated cost/experience relationship. The experience curve is not a natural law but requires a concerted effort on the part of managers to reduce costs.

The product life cycle

The concept of the product life cycle plays a fundamental role in strategic management. In simple terms the idea behind the concept is that industries and products go through stages, in a life cycle. The stage of this cycle at which an industry or product is at a given time has important implications for decision-makers. Four life cycle stages have been identified. The development stage is where a new product is introduced by one or a few firms, risks will be high and there will be high start-up costs in relation to sales. The second stage is the growth stage, where sales and profits increase and prices reduce. Price reduction is, in part, due to the combined effect of competition among firms and cost reductions. The third stage is maturity where sales growth is at a slower pace than previously and profits and prices reduce due to increased capacity. The final stage is decline. Market demand has to a large extent been satisfied and there is over capacity in the industry. Prices will remain stable or begin to fall along with profits and the particular product will probably change into a loss maker. Again, like the experience curve, the validity of the product life cycle concept to all products has been questioned.

Conclusion

This chapter has introduced the concept of strategy, a simple model of the firm with different layers of management focus has been presented and the chapter has explored the strategic management process. A series of strategic alternatives available to management has been discussed together with a series of typologies to describe firms' behaviour. The chapter concludes with a description of two other strategic management concepts, the experience curve and the product life cycle, although their relevance to the construction industry is open to question. Chapter 6 focuses on the implications of these ideas and concepts for strategic management in the construction industry.

Part III
Strategic Management Techniques

4

Futures and trends in construction planning

The song 'Imagine' by John Lennon captured the imagination of a generation but were the lyrics idle dreaming, wishful thinking, or a possible future for us all? They could be all three but such visions while of general interest need to be of particular concern to the strategic planner in construction organizations. What kind of future world there will be is a powerful determinant of the shape of the enterprise the planner is trying to plan. In the natural world animals and plants adapt to the physical environment; in the man-made world the construction industry and the firms which comprise it need to adapt to new environmental forces and changing circumstances. This sense of adaptability is not meant to be negative; people and organizations can, and do, shape the future. For the strategic planner it is as well to undertake an assessment of the forces at work which will influence the world of construction. The aim is to assemble the most accurate prediction of future conditions so that strategic planning can take place within reasoned projections. This chapter and the following chapter discuss techniques for analysing the future and its impact upon the construction industry and its component firms.

Futures

Let us first identify what is meant by 'futures' before turning to its application to the construction industry. 'Futures' emerged as a discipline after the Second World War and was used principally by the RAND Corporation. This was the first systematic approach to probing the future. The use of the word 'systematic' implies certain values of rigour and the use of 'scientific method' but, as de Jouvenal (1967) has argued, futures is not a science for it is based upon conjecture. This is important to the planner for it makes futures work accessible; expertise about the present is only one criteria for considering the future. However, as shall be seen, some 'scientific' techniques may be useful in understanding future possibilities. In general three types of futures can be identified:

1. Descriptive
   Here the work is visionary, and speculative. It is an imaginable future but nonetheless based upon conjecture.
2. Exploratory
   Here present trends are extrapolated into the future.
3. Prescriptive
   This is associated with a more proactive pattern in which the future is shaped by the choices one makes.

Naturally each of these sub-strands of futures work has a time horizon. Descriptive futures have the longest (for practical purposes only 30–40 years) with prescriptive futures being more susceptible to a short-term prognosis. In short one can exert a greater influence on events in the nearer rather than the distant future.

In these descriptions there is one common factor – uncertainty. The longer the time horizon the greater the uncertainty about what will happen and this uncertainty is amplified by the rapidly changing environment. One typical corporate response is to temporize. As Amara (1975) puts it 'to stay flexible, to monitor, to lay contingency plans, and to respond to the threat or opportunity of the moment may not be an altogether poor strategy'. However, there is a danger that the strategist may rely on such 'adhocracy' and it may become the dominant response then the firm is merely 'reacting' to events rather than attempting to shape them. Amara proposes three questions to be asked when addressing the future:

1. What choices do I have? (the art of the possible)
2. What do I know? (the science of the probable)
3. What do I prefer? (the politics of the preferable)

Such questions get to the heart of strategic planning by focusing on the objectives of futures. Underpinning these objectives is a guiding philosophy of change – that change is inevitable (if sometimes uncomfortable) – and the primary objectives of planners are to understand the basic processes of change and to identify and evaluate the underlying process of change. If planners were able to comprehend the dialectical pattern of the world then other objectives of strategic planning would fall into place. Thus they would be able to:

- Identify alternative futures and assess the level of uncertainty associated with each future.
- Establish and recognize through monitoring signals which indicate the development of particular futures in the construction industry. The objective being to minimize surprises for, as in the words of Milton Friedman, 'only surprises matter'.
- Set up numerous 'if-then' sequences which present the range of possible futures which may influence the construction firm. For example 'if' a government of one political hue is elected 'then' the workload for construction will be shaped by that political slant in the choices that the government makes.

Methods for futures research

How can strategic planners develop their thinking about the future? Three distinctive methods are available for futures research.

Models

A model can be built of the situation as we know it. Such models are often based on systems theory, in that several facets of the construction world are linked together to give a picture of the factors which are influencing our future position. Newcombe, Langford and Fellows (1990) see the construction process as being composed of 5 systems:

- The strategic system
- The information system
- The social system
- The organizational system
- The management system.

To quote Newcombe, Langford and Fellows:

> The strategic system performs the task of deciding and managing the long-term direction of the construction organization. The strategic managers of the business receive inputs in the form of market intelligence, assessments of the firm's current capabilities

and internal and external stakeholders' attitudes. These inputs feed a conversion process which decides objectives, generates optional strategies, evaluates, selects and communicates these strategies. The outputs of the strategic systems are strategic, administrative and operating decisions to facilitate the strategies. A control loop ensures that feedback of results against plans is achieved to allow modifications to be made if necessary.

The organizational system seeks to divide up or differentiate the work of the construction organization in a rational way, and to integrate or co-ordinate the activities involved. The inputs to this conversion process are environmental and organizational characteristics, current activities and stakeholder attitudes. The outputs will be a formal organization structure and an informal structure together with a complementary culture.

The social system's role input is people of various types and levels. Through the processes of motivation, group formation, leadership and communication, the system seeks to achieve an output of satisfied, committed and involved personnel.

The information system provides the lifeblood running through the arteries of the construction organization. Information from sources external to the business, together with data from inside the firm, is collected, sifted, sorted and disseminated to the other systems in the form of time, cost, quality, resource and statutory data. Information may be formally documented or verbally disseminated.

The management system is shown in Figure 4.1 as central to the whole organizational system. It occurs at three levels in the construction organization – strategic, administrative and operational – each with distinct functions. The strategic management role has already been described under the strategic system. The operational management role is about the construction production process. The administrative management role is usually referred to as middle management with responsibility for maintaining the organization and regulating its behaviour. At any level the management role involves making decisions, handling information and interacting with people. The way in which managers fulfil the role will depend upon the inputs they receive through their perception of the organization, the job itself, the team they work with and the task to be undertaken. Managers' perceptions will be coloured by their own personality, preferred management style and the demands, constraints and choices within the job. The outputs of the management system are primarily decisions and actions, but providing a motivating environment to facilitate the implementation of decisions is equally important.

Such models illustrate what we know and are useful for analysing the current position but many strategists have

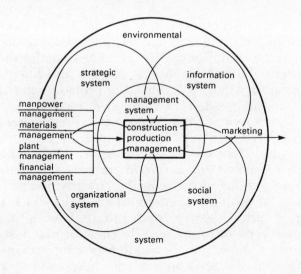

Figure 4.1 A systems model of the construction organization

Source: *Construction Management*. Volume 1. Newcombe, Langford & Fellows (1990)

agreed that such an approach is non-dynamic in outlook and as such is of limited use for forecasting. For example, a model of the industry cast in 1967 would show many different influences to those in operation in the 1990s. The whole nature of society has changed; it is less collective and more corporatist and workload, labour structure, and union power have altered dramatically. Hence a 1967 model would be of little value in shaping the firm to fit the construction world of the 1990s.

Trace
This approach seeks to predict the future by extending what we know of the past into the future. Taking our example of predicting the future from 1967, we may look backwards to 1947 to discover what changes have occurred in those twenty years and to consider whether those changes will continue. Does tracing the developments from the past suggest that the observed trends will almost certainly continue into the next twenty years or is there a more visionary approach, which poses a radical shift in the way in which buildings are bought, built and maintained?

Witnesses

The advantage of the past is that it is frequently documented and more recently the oral tradition of recording history has illuminated the past. But can the same be done for the future? To an extent the answer is yes, for the judgement of individuals or groups can be surveyed to provide a picture of the future. Care is needed here for we need to distinguish between 'preferences' and 'outcomes'. Preferences are not necessarily what is likely. For example, in the construction field pressure groups such as Transport 2000 or Friends of the Earth campaign for a certain 'future' and their visions would have various impacts on the construction industry, in the kind of work undertaken and the way in which the work was carried out. However, such groups have a 'preference' for a certain type of future and this may or may not come to pass. Futures, however, is about exploring and examining *possibilities* that the construction firm may want to promote, avoid or accommodate.

So far we have developed some general theories about how we can predict the future but to be of practical value the strategic planner needs some tools to work with. These are considered in the next section.

Techniques for strategic planning in construction

There are many techniques for forecasting future events based on known data. The roots of forecasting lie in operational research techniques and in particular there is a whole strand of operational research dedicated to forecasting methods. Of these, 'trends' is probably the most potent and yet most accessible technique for predicting what is likely to happen. This is not to deny the utility of techniques such as cost benefit analysis and decision trees but these are more often associated with decision-making when given certain assumptions. It is recognized that decisions taken will shape the future of a firm but they do not necessarily form part of a trend.

Trends – an overview

The basis of trend techniques is that the continuance of trends is used to predict the future. This approach can be somewhat unsophisticated. For example, consider the trends of the average height of buildings in Hong Kong. Naturally the trend is upwards (literally and graphically) but this is something which is easily measured. However, if the same technique is applied to the setting up of a construction claims consultancy division the results are more interesting. What will be the number of claims made by year 2000? Obviously many claims are settled privately and will not be recorded so some kind of index of claims is needed. Here, recorded 'litigations' may be the index upon which a trend can be set. However, trends need to be reviewed over time to be evident and may display certain distortions. These may be cyclical or seasonal. Also a trend may display irregular shocks. The example of construction output may be used to explain these features.

The data presented in Figure 4.2 graphs four years of construction output in the private sector (excluding housing). The undulations of the graph reveal that output is seasonal, with a rise in output occurring during the spring months. However, in the longer term the output may be cyclical. Figure

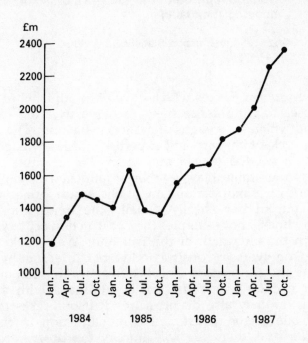

Figure 4.2 Construction output in the private sector, excluding housing (quarterly)

Source: Housing and Construction Statistics, HMSO

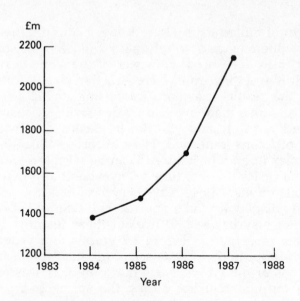

Figure 4.3   Construction output in the private sector, excluding housing (annually)

Source: Housing and Construction Statistics, HMSO

4.3 shows output figures which have been adjusted to eliminate the seasonal influence (i.e., averaged over the four seasons) and which show signs of cyclical behaviour. The reasons for such cycles may vary and expertise and knowledge of the industry is needed to evaluate them. For example, a large building programme may have been launched which pushes up output or a moratorium on public sector projects might depress output periodically. Finally the trend may record irregular shocks. For example, the construction activity associated with the aftermath of the Falklands War would appear as a 'blip' on overseas construction work carried out by British designers and contractors. This is obviously an infrequent and irregular event which must not be confused with a trend. Other factors may also distort a trend. If one takes the very high private sector investment in construction in the mid-1980s as a base then this will amplify the downward trend expected in the 1990s. Equally the growth in maintenance and refurbishment work in the 1970s looks massive when set against the pithy investment in maintenance in the 1960s.

Although it may be quite simple to identify a trend, it is

often more difficult to explain the reason for it. The most powerful part of trend analysis is the explanation of causal reasons for trends and the investigation of why variations in the trend occur.

An observed trend can serve as a catalyst to the planner for thinking about corporate direction and strategy. Certain situations are better suited to the use of trends than others. Obviously consistent historical data must be available and the data collected by government agencies can provide the basis for trend analysis. Output, broken down by type of work and region can be usefully trended as can employment by trade or region, and export markets in various parts of the world. Whatever trend is mapped, the planner must consider the following questions:

1. What are the consequences for the firm if the trend continues?
2. What are the consequences for the firm if the trend changes?
3. Which forces that are shaping the trend will continue and which ones are likely to change? What impact do these forces have on the firm?
4. What, if anything, can the firm do to alter the trend?

Some trend techniques

Several trend techniques are available and a sample of these is considered below, starting with the most simple and developing to the more complex.

Moving averages

Here the variations in data from year to year are smoothed out by trending the average value over a number of years and locating it in the middle of a cluster. Table 4.1 gives the figures for vacancies for bricklayers in the period 1977–87. The moving averages can be plotted as shown notionally in Figure 4.4.

This technique is quite straightforward and requires no further explanation.

Linear regression

This technique involves offering a straight line between a series of points. The line which best fits the points is the one which gives the smallest 'squared error'. This is the sum of the square of the vertical distance between the line and point.

Table 4.1 Vacancies for bricklayers, 1977–87

Year	No. of vacancies	Moving average
1977	2000	
1978	2400	
1979	2500	2300 (average of 1977, 78, 79)
1980	2400	2433 (average of 1978, 79, 80)
1981	2200	2366 (etc.)
1982	2000	2200
1983	1900	2033
1984	1800	1900
1985	1500	1733
1986	2000	1766
1987	2500	2000

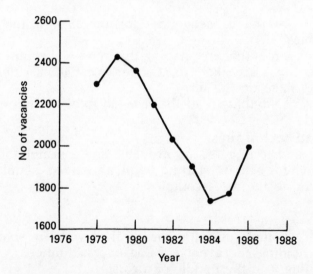

Figure 4.4 Trends for vacancies for bricklayers

Figure 4.5 illustrates this although it does not present 'real' data.

A further test of the fit of the line is to test for the 'r' of the line. This is the Pearsons' product moment correlation and can range from +1.0 to −1.0, both denoting a perfect fit with all points falling on the line. If the value is positive the slope of the line goes upwards, if negative it goes down. Figure 4.6 illustrates this point. In short, 'r' is a measure of how satisfactory is the fit of a straight line. A large 'r' demon-

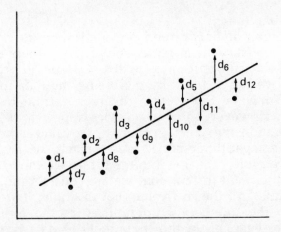

The best fit is one where the sum of the square of d_1 through to the square of d_{12} is the least value.

Figure 4.5   Line of best fit

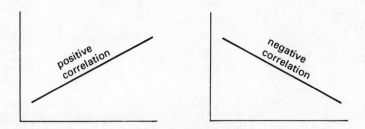

Figure 4.6   Positive and negative correlation

strates a good fit but a small 'r' should not be dismissed for it may simply be that the trend is linear but very wide year-on-year fluctuations occur. Alternatively there may be a trend but it is not linear, or no trend exists at all.

Curvilinear regression

If by inspection no linear trend is evident then the next move is to look for a curvilinear regression. This is where the trend is for an increasing rate of growth over time. If we look at Figure 4.5 we can see that by regressing the data in a linear way there may be too great a divergence from the line in later years. However, some trend does appear to be present. In this situation it is best to plot the Y values (the vertical axis) onto a logarithmic scale, thus making the graph more linear. If we project the line into the future we can extrapolate the arc to the point in time that we are considering and then take the antilog of the real value. For example, if we wish to extrapolate the number of apprentices in the industry for some future year, given the (hypothetical) data provided in Table 4.2, we would use the following procedure. Figure 4.7 shows the trend in the number of apprentices from 1977 to 1988. Figure 4.8 plots the logs of figures provided in Table 4.2.

Table 4.2   Vacancies for apprentices, 1977–88

Year	No. of apprentices	Log plot
1977	24000	4.3802
1978	19000	4.2788
1979	17200	4.2355
1980	15200	4.1818
1981	13800	4.1399
1982	12600	4.1004
1983	11000	4.0414
1984	10100	4.0043
1985	9000	3.9542
1986	8500	3.9294
1987	7600	3.8808
1988	7000	3.8450

If we wish to find the number of apprentices as at 1994 we extrapolate the log plot to give a log of 3.6. Taking the antilog of this figure we might expect, as shown in Figure 4.8, on the basis of historical data, that the number of apprentices will be 3,981.

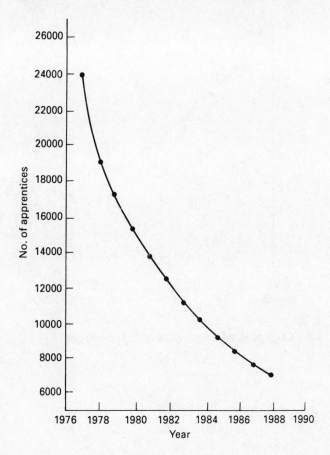

Figure 4.7   Trend in the number of apprentices (hypothetical)

Envelope curves
The use of these trend graphs are best demonstrated by an example set in the house-building industry. The environment is one where home ownership is growing at a rapid rate and the company has on offer an executive home in its range of houses. You are able to plot the cumulative units sold over time and after a while you decide to amend the specification to meet new market needs. This process is then repeated.

In this example we would expect the curves to be as shown in Figure 4.9. The trend in this type of executive home is not ascribed by any one type of house but by the tangential line above the tangent to individual trend lines. Trending in this way may be hazardous since it assumes that your judgement of the market quality will be as good in the future as it has

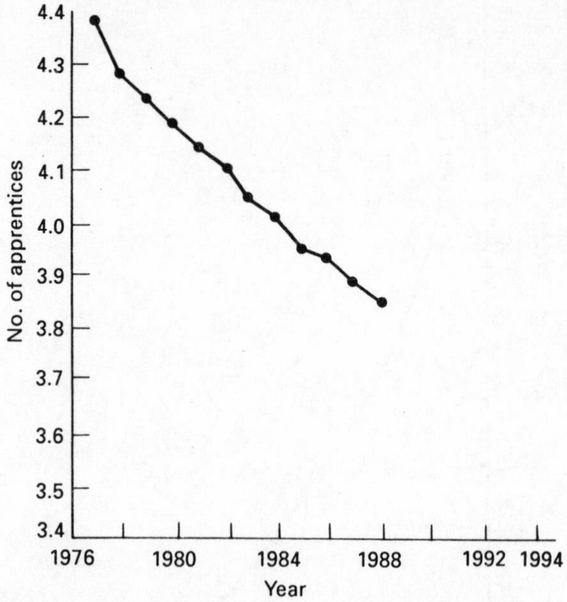

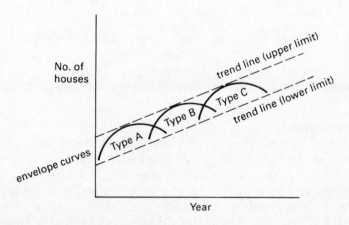

Figure 4.8 Log plot of the trend in apprentices

Figure 4.9 Envelope curves

been in the past. It also presumes that, in this case, the market for executive houses has not been saturated by the successes of the past and does not allow for new developments in technology, changes in fashion, credit adjustments, or other uncertainties in the housing market.

However, this technique can be useful for determining a trend in variegated markets and once the trend line has been found then projections can be made in the same way as for linear or curvilinear trends. Computer programs are readily available to undertake the calculations and presentation of data on trend lines.

The four techniques outlined here for projecting trends are simple and straightforward methods. Obviously there are certain prerequisites: historical data has to be available and staff have to be prepared to sift and, if necessary, index the data to make it presentable. But despite these requirements trending has the advantage of being a low-cost solution. Data can be drawn from sources such as the Housing and Construction Statistics and the Private Contractors Census published by the Central Statistical Office or from data about wages in the New Earnings Survey produced by the Department of Employment. Not only is the 'hard' data important but 'soft' realities may be just as crucial to the accuracy of the projections. Planners who are immersed in the history of a trend will be better placed to detect trends of the future, for research of a subject will enable the planner to spot causative factors which are instrumental in creating a trend. The explanation of *why* things are happening is probably of greater utility to the planner than the mere observation that they are happening.

It is also important to consider the time horizon of trends. We can extrapolate from the past into the future, but how far? The methods described here may be used for six months or 100 years, depending on the depth of data available but the question remains, will the future be a continuum of the past? For example, in New York in the latter part of the nineteenth century it was predicted that if the trend in the growth of horse-drawn carriages continued into the middle of the twentieth century then the whole of the city would be several feet under horse manure. Such projections obviously make no allowances for technological developments. There may also be natural limits on a trend, for example, in the construction industry the trend towards home ownership during the 1980s will surely reach saturation point. If a trend is to be sustained, a phenomenon known as the 'paradigm shift' must take place – old models and old ways of thinking about a problem are broken and are replaced with a new model. For example, Copernicus forced a paradigm shift by discovering that the earth rotates around the sun – the way people thought about the universe was 'shifted' by this discovery. In the construction industry the breakthrough could come from a number of directions, such as new materials, or the development of throwaway homes which people could replace as they do cars. No data is available for such projections and consequently one must look forward with an open-minded approach.

5

Portfolio management, Delphi techniques and scenarios

Business portfolio management

Portfolio management comprises a set of techniques which are often used by strategic planners to integrate and manage strategically a number of subsidiaries, often operating in different industries, that comprise the corporate whole. The larger the business the more likely it is there will be a number of operating units in existence which need to be integrated and managed strategically. One of the methods for achieving this which is most often discussed in strategic management literature is product market portfolio analysis (McNamee 1985, Howe 1986). Its use is primarily discussed in terms of large, diversified companies that have to consider many different businesses or Strategic Business Units (SBUs), with different products on sale in the market place or under development. In such a situation the strategic planning process can become complex and the main concern is to ensure a balanced range of businesses or activities (Johnson and Scholes 1988). In order to provide a structure and subsequent guidance for decision-making under these conditions a number of different techniques have been developed, using some form of matrix analysis. Underlying this analysis using portfolio techniques are the concepts of the experience curve and the product life cycle discussed in Chapter 3. McNamee (1985) indicates that portfolio management necessitates the determination of three fundamental characteristics of a product's or SBU's strategic position:

- Its market's growth rate;
- Its relative market share in comparison to the market leader;
- The revenues generated from the product's sales or the SBU's activities.

The Boston Consulting Group growth-share matrix

The fundamental characteristics of portfolio management can be represented pictorially. The Boston Consulting Group (BCG) growth-share matrix (Figure 5.1) is a widely reported example of this. The four cells of the matrix represent different decision situations.

Cash cows

These are the products or SBUs that generate more cash than they require to operate. They will have a high market share

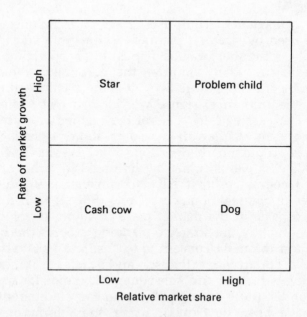

Figure 5.1   BCG growth-share matrix

Source: Tools and Techniques for Strategic Management, McNamee (1985)

but in a low-growth market. As they are cash generators this money can be utilized in other parts of the business.

Problem children or question marks
These activities require net cash inputs and are usually in a growing market where market share should be maintained or increased. The dilemma for the strategist is that the market is growing rapidly, the product or SBU has a low market share but requires substantial cash injections to allow market share to be built and thus allow the activity to become important for future profitability. The development of a project management service is an example of such an activity in the construction industry.

Stars
These activities have high market shares in fast growing markets and generate considerable amounts of cash. However, in order to maintain this position they also require considerable amounts of investment. Cashflow is, therefore, in approximate balance. Over time these activities could move into other quadrants on the matrix.

Dogs
Dogs have low market share in a low-growth market. McNamee (1985) and Wheelan and Hunger (1987) refer to two types of Dog, the former using the notion of 'kennel' to describe this situation. The 'genuine Dog' normally requires divestment. However, the 'cash Dog' may need careful management to generate some cash.

The BCG matrix has been criticized on a number of points which are outlined below (for further details see Jauch and Glueck 1988, McNamee 1985, Wheelan and Hunger 1987).

- The two-dimensional nature of the matrix is simplistic and the use of relative market share and growth rate may reflect only partly the determinants of a product's or SBU's success.
- The postulated strong link between market share and profitability may not always hold.
- High growth markets may not always be the best to enter. For example, project management has been suggested as being a high-growth market in construction (MAC 1985). However, there are considerable risks attached, not least that of liability. Substantial investment is required if an

organization is serious about offering the service and, in addition, personnel require a different orientation and set of management skills than many professions who purport to offer such a service are currently equipped with. Potential entrants may therefore face high entry barriers.

- The main reference point for the analysis is the market leader and no attention is paid to other fast growing but small enterprises.
- The matrix analysis does not represent adequately those businesses that are growing rapidly or are in a new industry in the business start up or growth stage.

In view of the limitations of the BCG growth-share matrix a number of other matrix type analytical techniques have been developed, for example, General Electric's 9 cell industry attractiveness business screen; the 12 cell product/market evolution matrix; the 4 cell BCG strategic environment matrix (McNamee 1985, Wheelan and Hunger 1987). Johnson and Scholes (1988) argue that portfolio analysis, using the preceding techniques, should not be viewed as a comprehensive method for evaluating different strategies but should be placed in the context of a preliminary step in raising the general awareness of managers about strategic issues. The following section relates the relevance of portfolio analysis to the construction industry and introduces the idea of 'Project portfolio management'.

Portfolio management and the construction industry

Two important issues have to be emphasized with respect to the application of the above concepts to the construction industry. First, many of these tools or techniques have been developed from a manufacturing industry base where the method of pricing and design/production processes differ considerably from that of contracting. Second, in large, diversified construction-related firms that have subsidiaries operating in a traditional manufacturing type of environment or those conglomerates with construction or property development subsidiaries, the use of portfolio analysis tools have an application at group or headquarters level (Ramsay 1989). However, the applicability of these ideas in the construction industry is compounded by the fact that the *product* in construction can be viewed as either (i) a completed project in the form of a building or other type of facility (in many cases a one-off for a particular client) or (ii) as a service. If the latter is true firms in construction may offer a portfolio of services. In the case of a contractor a portfolio of services may comprise design and build, management contracting and general contracting. In the case of a quantity surveying consultancy the portfolio of services could include feasibility studies, cost planning, production of tender documentation and post-contract final accounts and finally, project management. Additionally, there are problems surrounding the definition of markets in construction and subsequently in defining market share (Hillebrandt 1984).

For many organizations operating in the construction industry, such as a medium-sized regional contractor or a consultancy firm, the issue may not be one of managing different subsidiaries but the strategic management of different types of project. However, the management of different types of project also has implications for the larger organization in construction.

The management of a portfolio of contracts can be crucial to the success of the contracting company. Ball (1988) argues that profitability is dependent on achieving a balanced mix between projects that are underway and those being bid for. He sees the ability to diversify along the project dimension as a scale economy in the industry. Other advantages of project portfolio management include:

- The ability to enter markets easily without fear of retaliation. An issue of considerable importance in the manufacturing industries (Porter 1980).
- Access to new clients, tender lists and/or contacts through acquisition of other firms' project portfolios.
- Spreading risks over a number of projects to reduce the impact on turnover, profit and/or company operations of any one project. However, the nature of construction projects and the inherent risks attached may mean in practice that it only takes one project to destabilize a company's operations. For example, Morrell (1988) discusses in detail the impact of the problems encountered on the Kariba Dam that contributed to the eventual liquidation of Mitchell Construction.
- Market withdrawal is easier, especially for larger firms, since the commitment to any single market may be for the duration of one project only.
- Increased bargaining power with clients can be obtained due to a wider client and hence profit base.

The applicability of project portfolio management is not restricted to the contractor but also extends to architectural, surveying or engineering consultancies in the construction industry, especially now that competitive fees bidding is common. Unlike the contractor these organizations are not involved directly in the physical construction of a facility through the on-site production process. However, each of these types of firm derives its method of working, organizational structure and long-term business direction partly from the fact that a diversity of clients procure services on the basis of individual client project requirements. Therefore, many of the points highlighted above apply equally to consultancy organizations in construction.

Delphi techniques

In Greek mythology the god Apollo is afforded a special place for he was said to be able to foretell the future. He was reputed to have lived and worked from a temple sited at Delphi, some 170km north-west of Athens. What was special about Delphi was that fumes escaping from volcanic fissures were inhaled by acolytes who fell into trances and then made utterances interpreted by priests as predictions for the future. What has this to do with corporate planning? The drinks cabinet in the Board Room may be well-stocked and several directors may go into trances on occasion, but history can be of use. During the 1950s the RAND Corporation developed a technique for eliciting expert opinion by questionnaire and this survey technique was named the Delphi technique. An early user of the Delphi technique was the US military who asked experts to forecast where nuclear attacks would take place. By 1964 more peaceful use had been found, for a 'Delphi' was used by the US Government to try to predict the future of science and technology. Now Delphis are used in business to predict the future of an organization.

The Delphi technique can best be explained by using an example. Let us take a construction company who are trying to assess what the construction environment will be like in 2020. The first step is to assemble a number of experts in the company – not only directors but functional specialists such as accountants and engineers. When these participants have been briefed, the following question can be asked of them.

Question 1: In the current study a period of thirty years is being considered. It is possible that inventions not yet visualized could have a significant impact on the construction industry over this period. It has been seen that the industry has changed rapidly over the last ten years both in the technology and contract systems. What changes can you foresee in the next thirty years? List below the main breakthroughs that you think are urgently needed and which are feasible within the next thirty years.

A selection of items which may be submitted in response to this question are:

- The nature of the environment
  Sub-aquatic cities
  Building in space
  Building for space settlements
  Subterranean cities
- Ownership and contractual matters
  Design, build, maintain and refurbish contracts
  Industrial conglomerates having their own Direct Labour
    Organizations (i.e. vertical integration including construction services)
  Contractors required to put equity into projects
  Builders merchants become major equity stakeholders
  Totally integrated construction services
  No divorce of design and construction
- Construction techniques and technology
  Throwaway buildings (5-year life span)
  Entirely robotized construction
  Lightweight 'clip-on' materials
  Changeable environment (i.e. visualize a different environment and it will be given. For example, I need a break from work and I can organize my environment so that 'visually' I am somewhere else).

The next phase is to test the consensus of opinion amongst the expert panel. The suggestions can be put to them in the form of a question. Thus:

Question 2: Listed below are the breakthroughs suggested by the panel. Indicate as a percentage mark the probability of each breakthrough being implemented by the period of time indicated.

A completed questionnaire is shown in Table 5.1.

Table 5.1   A completed Delphi questionnaire

	% probability of event occurring in year					
	1995	2000	2005	2010	2015	2020
1. Environment						
Sub-aquatic cities	0	5	15	15	20	30
Building in space	5	10	40	80	100	100
Building for space settlements	25	100				
Subterranean cities	50	100				
2. Ownership and contracts						
Design, build, maintain & refurbish contracts	100					
Industrial conglomerates having their own DLOs	20	10	5			
Contractors' equity	0					
Builders merchants have equity stake	10	10	10	10	10	10
Totally integrated construction	40	50	60	70	80	90
3. Construction techniques						
Throwaway buildings	2	80	90	90	90	90
Robotized construction	10	90	100	–	–	–
Lightweight materials	50	80	100	–	–	–
Changeable environment	0	0	0	0	0	0

Following the panel's assessment of the projects the data collected can be analysed, based on a rolling forecast of when the events or possibilities are likely to occur. This can be presented in diagramatic form as shown in Figure 5.2. The probabilities supplied by the respondents are averaged and the highest probability of a date is signalled with the shortest time horizon being located earliest in the diagram. As can be seen the presentation appears as a bar chart with the events

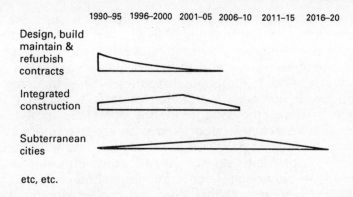

Figure 5.2 Probability of events occurring

considered to be the earliest possibility appearing first. This gives more of a sense of timing enabling adjustments to the possibilities of future events. The taller the apex on the triangle the more confident the reports are that this is likely to happen and the actual apex indicates when it is predicted to occur.

This approach is most useful when a problem does not lend itself to analytical techniques and is consequently subject to personal judgement. Also the approach is freed from the use of historical data as a guide to the future. By identifying and separating out the experts for this kind of research one can avoid the phenomena that often beset meetings of such people – meetings dominated by bandwagons, formal status divisions or strong personalities. The possible future environment for construction can thus be predicted, the process can be used as a communication tool and the results as a mechanism to tease out the pros and cons of various policy options.

In the example given a general approach has been used with 'experts' giving an opinion on all matters but obviously specialist groupings can be formed. Frequently these groupings are based around operating divisions within the company. For example, after an environmental framework has been established by a general 'Delphi' then specialist groups could consider futures in, say, house-building, international projects, industrial or commercial sector building, etc.

The Delphi technique is not without its difficulties. In many trials it has been found that the longer the planning horizon the greater the variation in the predicted date of an event. This position will be familiar to construction project planners who at the outset of a project are able to project the time of completion of foundations with greater certainty than the topping out ceremony. The time between the foundations and the topping out can encompass many events, which make the date of the topping out uncertain. Also, in using this technique, it has been found that there is a tendency to be pessimistic over the long term but optimistic in the short term. This tendency is associated with a sense of amortizing the future. Today's problems are those needing attention and tomorrow's problems do not assume much importance. Also respondents show a preference for simple and certain futures. In themselves these factors need not matter, for the aggregated opinion of the experts can provide useful insights for corporate planners and form a useful part of their techniques.

Scenarios

The following exchange was said to have taken place at a Cricketers Association (the professionals 'trade union') meeting. In a contribution to discussion Phil Edmonds of Middlesex and England is reported to have said, 'Let's postulate a hypothetical scenario'. The audience looked quizzically at him and David Lloyd of Lancashire noted, *soto voce*, 'It's all right, lads, he just means "let's pretend" '.

Is scenario planning just a fancy name for 'pretending'? If so, it has little value to the corporate planner, but scenario planning is more than pretending. In the words of Wilson (1978), it is an 'exploration of an alternative future', for, if we make certain assumptions, then the future may take a certain direction. Scenario planning can be described as follows:

1. Hypothetical – it exposes us to the numerous possibilities of the future.
2. Vague – it does not give detailed descriptions but provides a generalization of what may be.
3. Multi-disciplined – it is an overview which brings together all aspects of a society be they technological, economic, political, social, demographic or environmental. The scope of a scenario will depend upon what is attempted – a global scenario will be wider in the impacts it considers than a national scenario. Equally an industry scenario will be wider than one for an individual firm.

This section will focus upon the particular use of scenarios in companies and construction organizations. An essential building block of a scenario for companies and construction organizations is the 'trend', which was discussed in Chapter 4. Trends are naturally isolated from one another, each trend giving one set of information, but the scenario binds these into a complete, if hazy, picture. A scenario can be built and used as a framework for corporate planning, on which a construction organization will base its ability to adapt to a future changed environment. A scenario attempts to portray the future shape of the construction world and how the company can adapt to fit it. In a sense this is corporate ecology – the firm evolves to suit the environment in which it lives. This responsiveness to new environments implies a level of passivity on behalf of the firm yet planning suggests some level of proactivity. Not only does the construction organization react to the world but it can also assist in shaping that world. In global affairs, ITT (the US-based international communications company) played a significant part in shaping the political and, consequently, its own business future in Chile. In Britain the National Federation of Building Trade Employees (now BEC) contributed to the Conservative election victory of 1979 with its Campaign against Building Industry Nationalization (CABIN). These are broad, and some would argue less acceptable, examples of how futures can be shaped.

Whatever the purpose of the action which follows a scenario it is essential to have a planning framework from which to work. The objectives of scenario planning for companies are therefore:

- To set up forecasts of alternative economic futures;
- To set up alternative visions of the future;
- To identify branching points in the future which can act as early warnings for the company.

These objectives set the context for testing how well a company's products or services fit the various postulated futures. More specifically planners can test the outcomes of various company strategies in different future environments. This analysis leads to an assessment of the trends that may shape the future. This can be modelled on two axes: the probability of a trend occurring and the malleability of a trend. Figure 5.3 demonstrates the mapping of trends on these axes using four examples.

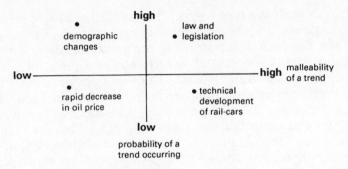

Figure 5.3   Some trends mapped

1. *Population and demographic trends*
   It may be that planners predict urban regeneration in the North of England with population shifts to this area. The planners see this as a high probability but can do little to shape the direction of this trend.

2. *Law and legislation*
   Planners may envisage changes in, for example, employment law and assess that the probability of these occurring is high. The firm can insulate itself from the effects of the changes by making certain strategic decisions, for example, subcontracting all work.

3. *Technical developments*
   Imagine that planners foresee that by 2000 the motorway and the conventional car will have been replaced by electro-mechanical cars which clip into an electrical rail fitted on a motorway lane. The rail governs speed and spacing between the cars. If drivers wish to leave the motorway they slip off the electrical rail and return to 'petrol power'. There may be a low probability of this happening but a firm could respond to this technical change and shape it through its own research into electrical transport systems.

4. *Increase in oil prices*
   This may be a possibility and it would certainly have an effect on a company's workload, however, it is an event which is outside the influence of the individual construction organization.

By mapping the trends which can influence the construction organization the scenario process identifies the initiatives that are needed and seeks to minimize the responses that corporations have to make. This thinking is based upon the formal planning logic that proactivity is preferable to reaction.

The process of formulating scenarios

The formulation of scenarios can be explained in more detail by describing a typical process, taking an international construction organization as an example. The first task is to select the areas about which scenarios need to be developed. The firm in our example is interested in the following global issues:

- The geopolitical balance of the world
- World economic development.

In the domestic market, however, it prefers to consider:

- The social framework of the future
- Political direction
- Economic futures
- Technological prospects
- Labour and demographic trends
- The legal framework for business.

The scope of the scenario is now defined. The second step is to historically review each issue with particular interest focused on recent history. This isolates the current trends in each issue. In our example the firm may see the world balance of economic order changing to redress imbalances between the wealth of the northern hemisphere and the poverty of the south. Consideration of the geopolitical issue may project *glasnost* to suggest a significant political integration of the world. This review leads to the third part of the process in which the future is projected from the detectable trends with 'probable' changes in each sector being postulated.

Thus far a picture is emerging but the planner has yet to assess the key change points which break away from the 'probable'. For example, if our scenario is for greater economic equality in the world, what are the key break points or factors which will decrease this trend? Finally, the planner has to assess the impact of these trends on the company. If we continue our example, the planner may suggest a strategy to meet expected construction demands in developing countries.

The steps taken to formulate a scenario generate a massive amount of information and some weeding out of the information is necessary to enable it to be manageable. A simple way of filtering the information is to quantify the probability of an event occurring and multiply it by the importance of the event to the company. Thus:

Significance of a trend = probability of an event × its importance to the company

The weighting of trends is crucial; an event may not be considered as highly probable but if it does happen then its effect may be catastrophic for the company. For example, if a mainstay of a company business portfolio is quarrying and processing materials for tarmacadam and a technological breakthrough, such as personal hovercrafts, enables personal transportation to operate without roads, then this would be catastrophic, even though the likelihood of the event is small. However, some events may be set aside altogether as not being influential on the firm.

The filtering process should enable the top fifty trends to be isolated. From here planners move on to use the technique of cross impact analysis.

Cross impact analysis

Events in history are seldom based around single issues although it may be convenient to presume so and say that A caused B. However, life is seldom so simple. Consider, for example, the events surrounding the start of the First World War. Schoolchildren are probably taught that the War started because an obscure Archduke, Ferdinand, was assassinated in a remote Balkan state. This single event was said to have triggered a war, but more complex, underlying issues could also be said to have been at work in the struggle for international markets among European nations. More recently, the tower blocks which were built in the 1960s were able to be built because of a fusion of technical capability, political need and encouragement, social needs and acceptance of such blocks, etc. In short, one event is an interaction of many others.

This technique can be illustrated by the example of a construction firm with a strong interest in the timber-framed housing market. Over the next twenty-five year period the corporate planners of this company isolate the following trends:

1. Acid rain has an increasing effect upon the tree crops in Canada and Sweden.

2. Canada and Sweden look to restricting the export of timber.
3. Legislation introduces statutory requirements to improve fire and sound insulation in timber-framed houses.
4. The decline in the timber-framed housing market is to continue.

Obviously there may be some links between these possible events. For example, acid rain makes restrictions on exports more likely; the decline in the popularity of timber-framed housing makes legislation less likely for there may be no purpose in legislating for a small market. These events may be classified so that several different kinds of relationships can be seen.

● Unrelated – one event occurring does not influence the probability of the second (for example, acid rain and legislation).
● Enhancing – the occurence of one event increases the probability of a second event either by enabling it to occur or by stimulating its occurrence (for example, acid rain and export embargo).
● Inhibiting – one event inhibits another (for example, fall in timber-frame sales and legislation).

However, it must be pointed out that the relationships established go beyond a simple pairing and that repercussive events may be set up. Also the strength of the relationship is important. In our example the relationship between acid rain and timber export embargo seems more likely than that between timber-frame house sales and legislation.

The impact of these different events can be analysed by setting up a matrix to demonstrate the way the probabilities work together. Such a matrix is illustrated in Table 5.2.

What are the chances of events 1 and 2 occurring together? We assign a probability of one event happening, for example, there is a 60 per cent chance of acid rain affecting the timber crop by 2000. If acid rain is going to reduce the crop then an embargo on timber exports seems more likely. The probability of both happening can be calculated by multiplying together the individual probabilities as shown in the Table.

To follow this through, reduced timber exports may increase the price of timber which in turn may be reflected in the cost of timber-framed housing. This will influence the price and depress the market. So the export embargo and fall

Table 5.2 Cross impact analysis matrix

	Probability of events occurring by 2000	1	2	3	4
1. Acid rain	0.60	–	0.18	0.24	0.30
2. Timber export embargo	0.30	0.18	–	0.12	0.15
3. Legislation re improved safety standards	0.40	0.24	0.12	–	0.20
4. Reduction in timber-framed housing market	0.50	0.30	0.15	0.20	–

in sales of timber-framed houses are connected by more remote events. The probabilities of all the events occurring can also be calculated. The probability of an export embargo being caused by acid rain is 0.18. The matrix can be then redrawn to show the relationship between the other variables. This is cross impact analysis.

After looking for any cross impacts, planners can proceed to write up the different scenarios. According to Zentner (1975) the scenarios presented must be:

- Credible (if not, planners have difficulty in developing strategies)
- Useful (relevant facts)
- Understandable (presented in a clear way).

In constructing a scenario for the construction organization it seems likely that the main elements to trend analysis would be:

- Demography – where people will live and work.
- Lifestyles – how people will live and work.
- Transport – how people will move around, where to and where from.
- Environment – what kind of built environment will people have?
- Technology – what technological advances can society be expected to make?

From such scenarios one can undertake sophisticated corporate planning in which 'what ifs' can be addressed. This imprecise science is important in setting up different potentialities for the company so that it can structure its operations to match likely scenarios of the future.

Part IV
Strategy Formulation

6

The development of strategic management in construction

The objective of this chapter is to integrate ideas about the nature of the construction industry environment and research on the management of contracting and professional consultancy firms with some of the concepts introduced in Chapter 3. The final section of the chapter draws together the various threads of this and earlier chapters to highlight major issues for developing a contingency model for strategic management in the construction industry.

Strategic management and contractors

Demand in the construction industry is created in a different way than in many manufacturing industries; the nature of competition in construction is determined substantially by the actions of the client. The evolution of the industry, shaped by the changing demands of clients, can best be traced historically. These historical developments effectively set the parameters within which current competitive forces act. However, in order to highlight phases of industry evolution in environmental terms, this section commences with an overview of how demand may impact strategic thinking. It is important for strategic analysis in construction to understand the relatively recent evolution of the industry and this importance can be illustrated by tracing the different types of environmental change.

Demand plays an important part in determining the nature of the construction industry with its effects being felt mainly in the long term as shifts between market sectors. In the early 1970s work by the Building Research Unit at Ashridge Management College indicated that whilst fluctuations in demand in the short and long term were substantial during the 1960s and 1970s they did not necessarily affect the efficiency and growth of individual construction firms, many of which had shown high growth rates. Data from the late 1980s also supports this view, indicating that rates of return have been consistently higher in construction than in manufacturing. Therefore, it appears that it is the general state of the economy rather than aggregate demand for construction that is one of the prime determinants of profitability in the industry. Additionally, data from the mid–1960s onwards reveals that there has been a counterbalancing effect between workloads for new buildings in individual sectors of the market. The net effect is that the overall aggregate workload for the construction industry is the sum of opposing movements in each sector. The trend for repair and maintenance (R & M) has been consistently upwards. The pattern of demand requires careful consideration in the development of any strategic options for a firm and any choice made within such a framework.

Types of environmental change

Three types of environmental change face managers in the construction industry. The first type is *operational change* where events are largely familiar and routine and can be handled by the use of experience. Under conditions of *strategic change* events will be largely unfamiliar and uncertain. This will require the synthesis of information about different events that have not been directly experienced. Thus insight and creativity will be required. *Competitive change* falls somewhere between the two and requires a combination of insight and experience. These different types of environmental change have had an impact on the construction industry since the end of the Second World War and have been experienced because of the effects of changes in demand. The patterns of change in the industry environment and their impact on industry evolution is now examined within the context of significant phases of development in construction since the Second World War.

The evolution of the industry

The industry environment of the 1950s and 1960s was characterized by stability, as reflected in high growth rates in construction output. Periods of recession only slowed the rate of increase. This rapid growth stemmed from the level of investment in infrastructure projects and house building. During this period of stability firms used their experience to identify those markets to which they were most suited. The thrust of the strategic management process was to invest in systems and procedures that would facilitate either control and/or integration within organizational structures and hence provide competitive advantage by focusing on internal efficiency. Strategists within construction firms could focus their attention on this mode of strategic behaviour because of the certainty that markets would not change dramatically. Market specialization occurred, not as any premeditated strategy, but rather through the use of managers' experience to identify types of projects which were successful for firms. The strategy formulation process was simple with little need for reference to the external environment. Lansley (1987) asserts that the implicit focus of contractors during this period was the utilization of a focus strategy based on cost leadership. The 1950s and 1960s were therefore characterized by operational change.

Ball (1988) asserts that the years 1968/69 formed a watershed for the construction industry. New orders in the sectors that had underpinned the earlier boom dropped dramatically as a result of the economic crisis of 1967, the devaluation of the pound and subsequent government policy. In the depressed conditions of the late 1960s contractors were forced to make rapid moves into new markets in order to avoid a sharp downturn in profits and as a consequence there was a merger boom in the late 1960s in response to falling workloads.

The 1970s were characterized by strategic change. The most important change was the sharp and persistent fall in demand. There was a sustained fall in total demand for construction of 30 per cent in some markets and 90 per cent in others. These changes were in complete contrast to those which had taken place in the preceding two decades. The dramatic changes in the environment of the 1970s meant that specialization had to give way to a strategy of breadth in order that firms could cope with the uncertainties and troughs in demand. These changes required a strategic orientation and a need for creative insight by senior managers. The problem facing contractors was the need to move away from a focus strategy to one of competing on cost within the context of a broad market base. The requirement for managerial decision-making and thus for company strategy was flexibility. A number of important strategic decisions were taken within firms during this period. Decisions taken in the 1960s to vertically integrate were reversed and companies divested themselves of businesses considered outside their 'core' activity. Portfolio management became important. The civil engineering sector, which had grown rapidly in the 1950s and 1960s, especially with motorway construction, faced a slowdown in growth in the 1970s and virtually all firms in this sector attempted to diversify.

A strategy based on steady internal expansion, of relevance in the 1950s and 1960s, was no longer an option in the 1970s. Acquisition was the only way of increasing market share. A merger boom occurred in the early 1970s as a result of a rise in new orders for certain types of work. However, by 1974 demand in every sector of the industry had plummeted. Takeover activity also fell dramatically and remained low until 1978. The crisis did not have a uniform impact for some contractors continued to make record profits but not on the magnitude of orders won. Many firms diversified overseas or adopted a 'wait and see' policy.

Additionally during the 1970s, takeover activity changed in terms of size of firm it involved. In the early 1970s takeover activity was dominated by small firms acquiring others and remained that way until the slump of 1974. Acquisition after 1974 was dominated by the medium-sized firms. This reflected, in part, the increased size of firm which resulted from the earlier small firm activity. From 1976 onwards large firms also increased their merger activity. By the 1980s some firms were so successful in diversifying that contracting represented only a small percentage of their overall business.

The issues confronted by managers in the 1980s were not unfamiliar and had their roots in events occurring between the 1950s and 1970s. The environmental circumstances of the 1980s included:

- Competitive changes in the environment largely due to long-term shifts in the structure of the industry and in client attitudes towards the industry;
- The increasing complexity of large building projects;

- The move away from traditional forms of building contract;
- Rapidly declining workloads with demand becoming unpredictable although there were short-lived recoveries in market by project type and location;
- A lack of skilled labour;
- A fall in overseas opportunities;
- New forms of project financing coupled with lack of public finance.

Lansley's (1987) contention, and one that presumably holds for the early 1990s, is that contractors are not well-versed in managing in such an environment. Therefore, in situations where demand becomes less predictable a policy of sub-contracting has considerable merit. This issue will be taken up later in regard to other organizational contexts.

Strategic alternatives

Chapter 3 has set out a series of strategic alternatives that are available to a firm's management and the preceding section has highlighted examples of where these options have been exercised. This section consolidates these within a broader framework.

One of the features of construction that has to be considered in the strategic decision process is that any one contract can form a relatively large part of a firm's annual turnover. Thus, the decision to commit resources to a particular project can be an important determinant of the profit or loss for any given year. Therefore, the resource capability of the construction firm sets the framework for strategic options such as, for example, growth. The Building Research Unit (1972) suggested that there is an upper limit to the growth which can be undertaken by contractors. Their empirical evidence from the early 1970s, based on a study of medium-sized contracting firms and regional subsidiaries of national contractors, indicates that a managed growth rate in the region of 10 per cent in real terms per annum is sustainable. Growth for contractors can be achieved in the following ways:

- Efficiency only. This requires no additional resources, turnover is maintained but there is a better use of inputs to achieve efficiency. Managers are concerned therefore with managing the internal dynamics of the contracting organization. This is a defender strategy, especially if contractors operate efficiently in niche markets.

- Growth in size only. This is a strategy of expansion where the attention of managers is directed more to the external environment in order to pursue opportunities rather than necessarily directing attention inwards to improve efficiency at the same time. This is a prospector strategy.
- Growth in size and efficiency. This requires attention to be directed first, outwards to the opportunities presented in the environment and second, internally to increase efficiency. This is an analyser strategy.
- No growth in size. A no growth or minimum growth strategy is essentially unstable. This has close similarities to the reactor strategy.

During the period of falling demand in the 1970s – a period of considerable strategic change in the industry – firms were unable to ride out the many environmental changes by having a high level of work in hand. Contracting firms were faced with three alternatives:

- To shrink – a retrenchment strategy;
- To contain the effects of the recession through their existing activities by increasing their internal efficiency and exploiting their markets more intensively – a strategy of expansion within existing markets;
- To enter new markets in terms of either project type, size or location – a diversification strategy requiring, in some instances, a redefinition of business scope.

Other options

The financial liquidity of contracting, via methods of payment based on regular interim valuations, offers contractors a number of options that are denied firms operating in continuous process manufacturing. These options comprise in broad terms, *financial management*, such as running down construction operations to reduce overheads, debt reduction, investing cash in the money markets, and *diversification*, which provide contractors with an opportunity to restructure their operations and hence spread risk. Diversification in construction can occur by the firm taking on work which represents changes in project size, type or location. Additionally, it can include the firm moving into materials manufacture or property development, that is, vertical integration or taking on board overseas work which represents geographic diversification or internationalization.

Empirical evidence indicates that market diversification appears to be the dominant reason for takeover activity in contracting. Diversification in construction is not a strategy to reduce industry capacity, as in manufacturing, as equipment and labour can be hired temporarily. Reasons for takeovers in construction include cheap acquisitions and entry into or strengthening of existing markets. Additionally, takeover activity in construction is linked clearly to phases of economic change in the environment and to changes in individual sectors of the industry. Furthermore, acquisition can help in the process of resource switching since the acquired company will have a standing with clients or their advisers in that sector of work, management expertise, a portfolio of contracts and membership of selective tendering lists.

International diversification is an example of geographic expansion, an activity which British contractors have undertaken for over 150 years. It is not, therefore, a relatively recent phenomenon. Diversification internationally in the 1960s was mainly perceived as an extension of the domestic market using colonial and military connections. There was a dramatic increase in overseas work in the 1970s, concentrated mostly in the Middle East. This provided a new source of market opportunity especially in the face of a declining workload in the UK. In practice, a relatively small number of contractors are responsible for much of the UK's overseas export of construction services. Ball (1988) suggests that in the UK only one or two contracting firms can be regarded as having a true international orientation. International diversification through mergers has played only a small part in contractors' strategies for overseas expansion. The ease of joint venture formation makes this particular strategic option a low priority.

Strategic management and the professions – architects and surveyors

During the last two decades the construction professions have gone through considerable changes. These changes are the result of a number of events and developments within the industry:

- The merger between the Institute of Quantity Surveyors and Royal Institution of Chartered Surveyors.
- The investigations of the Monopolies and Mergers Commission into the provision of services by architects and quantity surveyors and hence the instigation of the procurement of professional services through competition on price.
- The option of architects or quantity surveyors to be able to hold directorships in contracting companies.
- The redefinition of roles within professional groupings brought about by new methods of procurement and forms of contract.
- The increasing demands placed on the industry by clients.

Empirical studies

Within the last ten years there have been a number of reports and research studies that have addressed the roles, responsibilities and management issues which face architects and surveyors (e.g. Avis and Gibson (1987), Hillier (1979), Kelly and Male (1987), MAC (1985), Male (1984), Male and Kelly (1989), Male (1990), RICS (1984), and PRS (1987)). These studies reinforce and compliment material discussed in earlier chapters of this book. The main points to emerge are:

- Architectural practices during the 1970s shifted in size either towards the small or large end of the spectrum. This is also a characteristic of the surveying profession.
- Smaller architectural practices may have up to three times as high a proportion of private sector clients than larger practices although the latter may have more stable clientele.
- Many architectural practices have specialized involuntarily in particular building types as a result of relationships with particular clients. The tendency to concentrate on one particular building type may be more pronounced with large and small practices than with those of medium size. Specialization can limit the potential of a practice to adapt to changing patterns of demand.
- When dividing a project into strategic (dealing with the client end) and tactical (the construction end) areas, as firm size increases there is a tendency for architects to be more involved in the strategic end of projects.
- The role of the architectural technician has become well established. However, in the surveying field, especially

quantity surveying, problems of definition over the technician's role still occur.

- Clients believe architects should accept responsibility for the full range of normal and supplementary services and direct and coordinate all consultants.
- Clients believe architects have an inability to respond to changes or recognize the needs of the client.
- The prime threat to the architect in all areas except for design is seen as coming from the chartered surveyor.
- For the surveying profession as a whole, the markets it serves are diverse and clients are changing their buying behaviour with respect to surveyors' services. Additionally, there is increased competition, not only between surveying firms but also with other professions.
- Surveyors' markets are characterized by a transition from growth to maturity and from regulation to deregulation.
- Large quantity surveying practices offer a relatively narrow range of services. It has been suggested that such practices should broaden their scope of service provision or be managed as decentralized entrepreneurial units – a direct application of the strategic business unit concept introduced in Chapter 3. Additionally, medium-sized general practice firms have been advised to opt for growth, either through internal expansion or acquisition.
- The quantity surveying profession is now offering many more services than just preparation of tender documentation and post contract services – the traditional core business of quantity surveying. However, the core business activity still accounts for approximately 70–75 per cent of workload.
- In general, it is the leading edge of the quantity surveying profession, some 20 per cent of practices, that are involved in the provision of services outside the core business. The addition of new services, such as project management and value management, will be taken on board by these practices.
- The use of sub-contracting within quantity surveying may force changes in the 'form' that the profession takes and determine future developments in the control of the profession.
- The majority of general practice firms are not concerned with a future orientation. All types and sizes of firms have difficulty in implementing strategic planning partly because of an inability to take a broad view of the firm

and its markets. However, operational management appears well developed, through the use of regular reporting procedures and meetings.

- 65 per cent of general practice income comes from existing clients but clients are increasingly exercising choice and widening their service procurement options.
- Competition among architects, surveyors and engineers will occur increasingly at the boundaries of a profession's skills and knowledge base – where services are prone to develop and hence overlap.

An analysis of strengths and weaknesses – architects and quantity surveyors

Tables 6.1 and 6.2 provide an assessment of the strengths and weaknesses of architecture and quantity surveying, based on the reports produced by MAC (1985) and PRS (1987). In some instances, these strengths and weaknesses are the mirror image of each other, representing the aggregate views expressed by different clients in contact with these professions.

Towards a contingency model for strategic management in construction

This section draws together the themes introduced earlier in the chapter and provides additional supporting material to integrate this within the framework of issues which need to be considered in the strategic management of construction.

The business environment of the construction industry has gone through three major changes since the Second World War, namely from operational through strategic and finally, to competitive change in the 1980s and early 1990s. The nature of demand and client-induced changes have had a substantial effect on industry evolution. However, depending on the nature of the firm, environmental pressures have been felt differentially. This differential effect will be explored in greater detail below.

In terms of trends in demand, there has been a long-term move away from public sector funding of construction projects. However, workload trends in the private sector cannot be viewed with such a long-term perspective and have con-

Table 6.1 Architecture: an analysis

Strengths	Weaknesses
Design ability is important for client choice.	Seen by clients as designers only.
Normal and supplementary services sought by clients have a strong design input.	An inability to adapt to alternative procurement methods has meant that fee income is lost through competition to other professional groupings.
Early advice on developments.	Chartered surveyors are seen to have a better understanding of property development.
Their range of skills supports the lead consultative role.	A lack of business acumen and poor marketing of services.
	Lack of attention to project cost control and timely provision of information.
	Traditional role as team leader has gradually been eroded as project managers are now being seen as the naturally evolving lead consultant.

Table 6.2 Quantity surveying: an analysis

Strengths	Weaknesses
Identification with client needs and value for money.	Lack of identification with client needs and poor value for money with respect to service provided.
Early involvement in projects.	Narrow advice and lack of consideration of cost implications of alternative solutions to client problems throughout the project life cycle.
Senior QS contact.	Lack of awareness of management principles. Lack of commercial aggressiveness.
QS is proactive and advice is accurate and action-oriented, especially in early stages of the project.	QS is passive or reactive with a slow delivery of and inappropriate service.
Advice on services engineering is provided.	Lack of advice on services engineering.
The service provided is in balance with the needs of the project at all stages in its life cycle.	The service provided is too detailed and inappropriate for the stage of a project.

siderable short-term variability. Under the Conservative government's policy of targeting increased use of private sector resources in construction and with the continued likelihood of shorter-term variability in workload within the private sector, the levels of uncertainty facing contractors in the 1990s is likely to increase. This is especially true if, over time, the industry workload from private sector investment, as a percentage of total workload, continues to increase in importance. The extent to which a Labour government, if and when elected, would alter this balance remains to be seen. Additionally, since sectoral variability in construction markets appears to be considerable managers will be called on increasingly to use skills in the shifting of organizational resources in order to take advantage of these sectoral changes. The impact of this at the strategic level is the need for increased ability to read and respond to changes in a more variable business environment and for firms to be able to cope with such changes. Ball (1988) contends that this shift towards the increasingly speculative nature of demand will mean that medium-sized construction firms in economically depressed regions of the country will be worst hit. In the medium to long term, therefore, on the assumption that these patterns continue, the present trend in the industry towards either smaller or larger enterprises is likely to be exacerbated.

Strategy and contractors

The implications of these trends for the strategies of contracting firms, in particular, are clear. First, specialization in one sector could be fraught with considerable difficulties since work shortages may be inevitable. Second, the counter to this is to spread risks and operate in a number of sectors. However, the technologies required in different sectors may be different. This favours the large contractor who has the resources to cover such a range of work. Third, with R & M having a consistent upward trend work opportunities in this sector are therefore considerably better. However, the methods of working and contract management requirements are different for R & M than for new building projects. Increased resources for training may be required to cope with the additional skills needed to capitalize on these market opportunities. Additionally, the scale of work operation for R & M favours the small contractor. Straddling different industry sectors typifies the strategic behaviour of the largest construction firms in the industry. These firms emphasize particular sectors in accordance with current management strategies. In addition, if, as Ball (1988) contends, contractors act in a merchant-producer role, this, combined with their market power, allows them during periods of slump to pass costs onto others. Workload flexibility puts contractors, therefore, in a strong position over sub-contractors, materials suppliers and building workers and provides them with the ability to maximize sectoral market opportunities.

The net effect of client pressures has been a demand for a greater diversity of services and ways of interfacing with the industry, especially for contractors. One of the major issues for clients in the 1980s was that of quality in construction. This concern for quality has affected not only contractors but also the professions. For contractors, the main issue highlighted in this chapter has been the use of diversification to counterbalance falls in sectoral demand by switching into different sectors to take advantage of their upswings. The financial flexibility of contractors allows them to diversify either through internal expansion or acquisition.

Strategy and consultants

In the client/professional interface, clients of the surveying profession have blurred the distinction between professional services, based on formal learning, and commercial services, based on the use of experience and therefore not requiring expertise in order to sell them. Architects, traditionally operating within a lead consultant role, are increasingly seen by clients solely as designers rather than as designers and managers of the building process. Weaknesses in the surveyors' position stem from an over concern with technical skills at the expense of business and commercial skills. This latter charge has also been levelled at architects.

In combining the empirical evidence (as quoted on p. 94) from architecture and surveying the following picture emerges. A restructuring, similar to that in contracting has occurred in the size of consultancy firms, namely, a polarization towards small or large organizations. Firms are having to respond to a diversity of market and client types with approximately 65 per cent of workloads coming from existing clients. However, due to the restructuring processes within professional markets, larger practices have a more stable clientele with the greatest variability being experienced in the small-firm sector. Firm size also has an impact on the form of pressure exerted by clients. As firm size increases professionals become more involved in the strategic end of projects and have more interaction with clients. Empirical evidence from the late 1970s indicates that due to client demands specialization by project type is probable in both large and small practices but not in medium-sized firms. Historically, client pressures appeared to be forcing consultancies towards niche strategies although with the introduction of fee bidding this process may well be reversing. Fee bidding may force some consultancies towards a generalist orientation. Evidence from both the surveying and architectural professions indicates that a production core of technicians is probable, especially as firm size increases. For surveying, interdisciplinary competition among firms is likely to increase, leading to a redefinition or virtual disappearance of boundaries between divisions of surveyors. Innovation is occurring in the leading edge of the professions, some 20 per cent of practices. This would indicate an increased need for flexibility. Surveyors are turning to sub-contracting out work to other practices to even out workload problems. Additionally, surveying firms appear to be adept at operational management but not at strategic management. Based on empirical evidence, the same could be postulated for architectural firms. In architecture, competition in the main comes from the surveying profession, except in the area of design, and as such skill substitution between the professions is apparent in many areas. Thus two forces – client procurement practices and competitive pressures – are acting in combination to force architects towards the design end of the building process. Much the same argument could be put forward for consultant engineers, from whom quantity surveyors are increasingly taking over the financial control aspects of engineering projects.

The picture that has emerged from this analysis is that the strategic decision-makers of firms in the construction industry are facing different types of pressure. Those in contracting, traditionally acting in a competitive environment, are now operating different types of diversification strategy in response to historical changes in their business environments. The professions are operating within business environments characterized by higher levels of competition, not only between professions but also within professions. Therefore, strategists within professional consultancy firms are being forced to make strategic decisions not only about how to cope with competition but also about how to respond to a business environment requiring diversification strategies. They are also now considering boundary spanning activities, acquisitions and mergers, and sub-contracting. The business environments of these firms require the development of strategies and management skills previously characteristic of only a contracting firm. Underpinning this analysis is the requirement of strategists in all types of business to handle change effectively.

The management of change

Lansley *et al.* (1979) in their study of regional contractors or regional operating units of national contractors, suggested that some strategists had adopted priorities that were counterproductive to the effective handling of change. Management orientations found to be most often lacking were those concerned with human resource management or a corporate perspective. Additionally, where a lack of people orientation was found there was also higher levels of organizational politics. It was this preoccupation with objectives associated with organizational politics that led to low staff morale and lack of organizational effectiveness. Additionally, the requirement for boundary regulation, i.e., the interface between the firm and its immediate or task environment, was greatest in medium-sized firms. Where the need for boundary regulation was understood by strategists a marketing function had developed. However, in those instances where this development had not taken place it was more an issue of lack of understanding of how to undertake it by strategists than a lack of appreciation of the need for it.

By the early 1970s the largest firms in the sample of contractors studied by Lansley *et al.* had identified the need for and had developed planning systems. However, the issue in the mid-1970s had become one of how best to use these systems. Moreover, in situations where a longer-term adaptive mode was required to instigate full corporate planning, some companies had 'regressed' in the sense that they had reverted to efficiency planning through a simple budgetary framework. Put simply, these companies had misjudged the requirements of the business environment in terms of the appropriate planning mode. As a consequence, there was a need for managers in contracting firms to overcome the notion that budgetary control was synonymous with the corporate planning process. Additionally, at a time when firms needed to make the best use of people with immediate market knowledge – their senior regional managers – planning was centralized, the net effect being that these companies moved away from direct market sensing and contact. These companies needed to take on board the fact that corporate planning provides an opportunity to systematically evaluate alternative future actions and solutions.

It could be stated that managers' responses to environmental changes are affected by the extent to which they have previously considered or familiarized themselves with problems presented by the business environment. Familiarization is assisted particularly by the use of formal planning processes and the development of objectives for the firm. The consideration of alternative courses of action by strategists facilitates flexibility. Characteristics representative of flexible firms have been identified by Lansley *et al.* (1979);

- Staff perceive senior managers to be committed to clearly defined and stated objectives which are directed at achieving well defined market goals. Strategists have, therefore, a clear 'vision' of the future direction of the firm.
- There is a concern for the welfare of staff.
- There is a close association between the management style adopted by senior managers and that preferred by staff, i.e., there is an internal consistency reflected in the organizational 'climate'.
- There are high levels of staff morale and job satisfaction.
- There is a history of effective change management.

Change and organizational structure

As a result of his historical analysis of environmental periods in the industry and the consequent changes that these have brought about in the structure of contracting firms, Lansley (1987) concludes that as the environment of the 1980s stabilized, management styles moved towards task orientation with less emphasis on people skills as individuals' roles in their organizations became more clarified.

The nature of professional consultancy work in construction, in comparison to that of contracting, may highlight the need for different types of organizational structure and hence responses to the business environment. Empirical evidence of architectural practices indicates that there are three types of organizational structure: the 'simple hierarchy', where relationships are vertical rather than lateral; 'organic', where structures are relatively unhierarchical but involve a large number of vertical and lateral relationships; and 'mixed', where there is a marked organizational tree structure but this is modified in part by lateral relationships. Private sector practices, of more relevance here, can be characterized by either organic or mixed organizational structures. The smallest practices tend towards being strongly organic but even the largest practices with some form of tree structure can have overlays of the organic structure. It can be concluded that in the private sector there is a constant emphasis on fluidity of practice and the importance of informal relationships. The overriding need is to meet those changes in the workload primarily induced by the business environment. The informal and not the formal organizational structure appears to be the key in private sector consultancy practices.

Since the competitive fee bid system has become the norm for procuring professional services, consultancy firms, like contractors through their estimating function, are now being forced into considering boundary regulatory roles such as 'marketing' and 'proposal preparation'. Eventually the counterparts to contractors' estimating and marketing departments will emerge more forcefully within consultancies of different sizes as environmental change compels them to adapt in the medium to long term. Many of the larger consultancy organizations, especially those operating internationally, already have a clearly defined marketing role, indicating the importance of boundary spanning activities for them.

Conclusion

The phases of industry evolution together with significant client pressures have set the parameters within which current strategies in construction have to be planned. Environmental pressures and demands have had differential impacts on contracting and professional firms. As a consequence, while there are similarities emerging between the general strategies adopted by contractors and consultants, the skill and knowledge bases from which these organizations have to confront the changes now occurring in their business environments are totally different. The final chapter will explore these in more detail.

7

Strategic planning in contractors' organizations

The foregoing chapters have developed ideas about the process of strategy formulation and how strategies can shape corporate performance in construction. This chapter examines, through case studies, how strategy is developed in five construction organizations. The case studies serve to illustrate the various strategies available to construction organizations and the chapter concludes with some comparisons of these companies. Much of the fieldwork was undertaken by postgraduate students who used material published by Taylor and Sparkes for the first case study.

CASE STUDY 1: A large international building and civil engineering company

Background
This company is seen as a blue chip construction company and its activities cover the full range of construction services in the UK and internationally. Currently it has a divisional structure with each division being an autonomous profit centre.

In the early 1960s a formal means of corporate planning was introduced to the organization. The basis of this early introduction of planning was the formalization of the guiding principles of the organization. In short, the main objective was to create a public company but one where controlling interest could not pass from the family dynasty. This objective was supported by principles which sought 'fair play' in terms of protection for creditors, customers, investors and the workforce, and which provided a framework for planning. The firm had gone public in the early 1950s and with the family interest secured the strategic objective was to attract investment to generate growth. This growth continued through the 1950s and in the early 1960s the firm experienced record profits. The Board then decided that future growth depended upon a formalized strategy.

The company objectives
The company has both economic and non-economic objectives. The main economic objective is to maintain its share value by satisfying investor expectations for dividends. Additional to this is the desire to consolidate the firm's presence in existing markets and diversify into new, promising markets. In the words of the current chairman, the company aims 'to be robust, energetic and profitable'. The strategy developed to ensure profitability is based upon growth in core divisions which provide major profit contribution. New markets are also sought into which the firm can diversify. The core divisions operate in highly competitive markets and the strategy is to encourage them to act in an entrepreneurial way. This creates a setting whereby the organization can respond to new demands and new markets by calling on the

expertise developed in the core divisions. This approach feeds a strategy of diversification which is further supported by a takeover strategy to accelerate diversification where necessary.

These are the economic objectives but there are also non-economic aims. The organization seeks to maintain a high reputation with clients and fair dealings with suppliers, subcontractors and employees. A strong commitment to employee training is evident and is conditioned by two factors: first a public recognition that its people are vital to its success; second it seeks to be in the vanguard of training activity in the construction industry. The firm continues to stress the importance of training and career development opportunities for its staff. Finally the organization is committed to community projects as part of its general social responsibility.

The planning process

The recognition of the need for planning was matched by the recognition that in-house expertise was not available. Consequently long-range planning specialists from the USA were hired to assist the company in creating the corporate plan. In order to create a plan each division within the company was asked to prepare a five-year plan and the objective of each plan was to produce, for each division, a 20 per cent return on capital. For the first planning period profits would be invested in a property portfolio which would provide share dividends. Experience of the first five-year plan showed that managers were being optimistic in their forecasts of turnover and profit and the main reason for this was the downturn in workload. As the second plan came into fruition the planning process was refined to take into account the influences of the external environment. The first plan had failed accurately to judge the political and economic climate and had assumed a continuum of the trading conditions of the 1950s. Therefore the company had not been prepared for depressed results following the downturn of the early 1960s. The first five-year plan was prepared by establishing a general objective and then letting the operating units build the plan. This 'bottom up' approach had the advantage of educating line managers in the necessity of planning. Subsequent plans were prepared centrally and fed to the divisions, and in this way an overall view of the influence of construction cycles could be appraised and related to the targets of the divisions. Thus the planning process changed from 'bottom up' to 'top down'.

The time-frame for planning also changed. A strategic review, which entails long-range forecasts, has a range of 10–15 years. Within this the company has short-term plans which view the next two years. The distinction between these plans is important; the strategic plan serves as an instrument for shaping the company to meet the needs of the construction environment of the future; the short-term plan is the operational plan for converting policy into action and acts as an instrument for exercising control over the performance of the divisions. The long-term strategic plan is prepared by the central planning department and agreed by the main Board, whilst the short-term plan is prepared by the operating units of the company. These short-term plans have to be set within the assumptions established by the long-term plan. Such assumptions provide the unifying ideology of the expected directions of social, political and economic trends. In this way the 'top down' approach is blended with the 'bottom-up' pattern of planning. The short-term plans are converted into schedules of action which are tasks which need to be undertaken in the next twelve months. The financial part of the plan is put into an overall budget which is prepared quarterly for the first year and annually for the second. The second year finance plan is used as an instrument of resource planning and acts as an early warning device of resource scarcities or surpluses. This plan is reviewed quarterly and revised as necessary.

CASE STUDY 2: A medium-sized construction company

Background

This company was formerly a household name in the civil engineering sector of the industry. The company was first incorporated in the early years of the twentieth century and the firm developed to take a prominent position in a regional construction industry. In the mid-1960s the company was taken over by a large civil engineering contractor and, with one minor change of nomenclature, continued in its present form until it was reconstituted in the mid-1980s.

Strategy formulation background

The current strategy needs to be considered in the context of the condition of the company when it was reconstituted in the 1980s. When the company was re-established it had continuing problems in recovering debts from overseas projects including a considerable bad debt provision for a contractor in receivership. These conditions led to the reconsideration of the strategy of the company, involving a withdrawal from some of the international market places and a new focus being placed on Far Eastern contracts. African activities were concentrated in countries where funds were remittable and politics were stable. This geographical reassessment was coupled with the central question 'what business should we be in?' Prior to the mid-1980s the firm concentrated on civil engineering contracts and due to the dearth of such work the firm refocused its efforts on to management contracting. This change proved difficult to implement for one main reason: clients were reluctant to offer the firm management contracts since it was still strongly identified with its civil engineering background. Consequently, early efforts to break into management contracting were unsuccessful. A Development Company was created to overcome the problem and to develop opportunities for the newly reorganized company. The advent of the firm as a management contractor posed further problems – management contracting offers low returns for confined risks and the firm found that civil engineering profits previously obtained by the company outstripped current returns. However this disappointment was tempered by the lower capital requirements of management contractors compared to civil engineering.

The company objectives
The company objectives are shaped by the capital structure of the company. All shares are held by the directors of the company and it would appear that profitable trading is the sole objective. No community-based objectives could be detected. This profit-centred objective has led the firm to seek out low risk activities with modest returns. This objective may be a reaction to the relatively high exposure experienced in the overseas market. Short-term objectives relate to company restructuring with a diversification from civil engineering to management contracting. This has been supplemented by a desire to emphasize negotiated rather than competitively tendered contracts.

The planning process
The Board of Directors are responsible for the planning process. It would appear that a fairly formal process is in operation. A group of directors undertake a SWOT analysis and this is then prepared as a two-year plan. This is converted into operating plans which are monitored on a monthly basis.

CASE STUDY 3: A small national contractor with a specialized market niche in design and build construction

Background

This company is one of the largest privately-owned construction companies in the UK. The company was founded in the early 1950s by three members of a family. During the 1950s it operated as a small building company in the London area but in the late 1960s the company was awarded its first design and build contract. This was an important milestone in the development of the company and it has developed this side of the business to such an extent that it represents some 60 per cent of the £120M turnover. Much of the design work is undertaken within the organization so that clients are provided with an integrated construction service. The design service is provided by a wholly-owned subsidiary which operates on a multi-disciplinary basis using a high degree of computer-aided design and drafting.

The company has other operating divisions and these include a management contracting division, a joinery company and until recently a building services installation firm. The workload is focused in the private sector and the company tackled work for local authorities, civil engineering projects and overseas contracts. Recently it has withdrawn from the speculative housing field. The majority of its workload is drawn from industrial, commercial and retail developments with a small section coming from a specialized market niche in laboratory construction. Remarkably the profile of clients is constant with the firm's claim that 60 per cent of current contracts are with previous clients.

The company objectives

As far as can be determined the company has two overriding objectives. One of these is internal, in that it has typical economic objectives, the other external in that it aims to have complete identification with client needs. No explicit social or community objectives could be identified.

The planning process

The strategic planning process of the firm is influenced by its size, its form of corporate leadership and its management style. The company is a large medium-sized firm and this influences the way it is managed. The form of leadership exercised is entrepreneurial as the founder of the business is responsible for all strategic decisions. This form of corporate leadership lends itself to an autocratic managerial style with all significant decisions being taken by the chairman who may (or may not) consult with the managing director and financial director.

This style of management has meant that the strategic planning process is not formalized in any way and consequently the process is intuitive and opportunistic. This process has worked for the company as the strategy of avoiding public sector contracts insulated it against large declines in public sector work. Conversely its preference for private sector contracts has given it some impetus during the 1980s. However, as private sector investment declines in the wake of rises in interest rates it remains to be seen if this will promote a preference for more formal planning methods. The evidence seems to suggest that a more formalized process is envisioned for the future. The firm has recently appointed a corporate planner who reports directly to the chairman and this development hints at a move away from the entrepreneurial style which has dominated the company over the last twenty years. The injection of formal planning will still mean that the process is conducted as a 'top down' exercise with little involvement of the operating divisions.

CASE STUDY 4:   A medium-sized residential development company

Background

This company, which began life in the late 1970s, is seen as an important niche builder in the retirement field. The genesis of the firm was stimulated by the publication of a Government Consultation paper on the housing needs of elderly people. This paper drew attention to the dearth of housing provision for the elderly which hitherto had been provided by local authorities. However, such provision was only supporting the needy and left a gap in the market for housing for the elderly with means.

The two principals of the firm spotted this niche in the market and used their experience of the speculative housing market to make an entrepreneurial response to the document. The principals had a small site on the south coast which was too small to develop in a conventional way so they built a block of leasehold 'sheltered' units. Demand far exceeded their expectations so they shaped their business to meet this demand. The firm expanded and in order to create capital for growth made its debut in the Unlisted Securities Market in the early 1980s. The firm became a star performer in the USM and graduated to a full stock exchange listing eighteen months later.

The firm has some twenty offices throughout Britain and has expanded to other parts of Europe. Until the housing slump of late 1989 the firm employed 2000 personnel, mainly administrative and managerial staff. The slump led to retrenchment and offices have been closed and staff laid off.

The company objectives

Superficially the company is driven by growth of turnover and profit. To this end it has been successful but these are the product of careful selection of the market niche and of the values which create sales; striving for excellence in the care of the retired person and ensuring that the customers are happy. This view expresses a strong commitment to quality in order to enhance the company's reputation in the market place. This quality objective is articulated frequently and at length by the senior management of the company. Employees are expected to maintain a close relationship with customers to better understand their needs and expectations and these customer requirements are converted to profit by providing quality care for retired people. Thus quality is a dominant objective within the company and finds expression throughout the organization from the Board of Directors to the subcontractors on site.

The planning process

The planning process is characterized by a 'power culture' and the company and its approach to corporate planning is typical of entrepreneurial companies in their growth stage. The direction of the company is largely dictated by the managing director. This highly personal style is maintained by the formulation of a corporate leadership image promoted by company publications and the presentation of the managing director as a role model for the managers. While the strategy formulation is created and disseminated by the individual he is helped by outside consultants who provide research services to explore the market for the services that the company offers. Also, as part of its strategy, the firm has developed personnel profiling using psychometric tests to enable it to select staff who fit in with the managing director's vision of the future.

The firm's strategy has been based around the identification of a market niche and then opportunistically exploiting its lead within this niche. The difficulties in retaining this strategy is that others may follow and fierce competition may ensue. This is, in fact, what has happened and returns for this company are being squeezed by competition and the sea change in the housing market following the imposition of high interest rates.

CASE STUDY 5: A medium-sized regional contractor (part of a larger construction group)

Background

This company is one of eleven autonomous subsidiaries of a large construction group. The company was taken over by the group in the late 1970s after a traumatic period when the company had gone into voluntary liquidation in the wake of the recession earlier in the decade. The reasons for this failure are interesting in themselves. At the time of the liquidation the company was heavily involved in property development and the secondary bank collapse of the early 1970s took the company into liquidation. At that time the company was not diversified and had little strategic nous. Opportunism was the favoured manner of operation. The company is now in a strong position within a buoyant region of the UK and has a major presence in building, civil engineering and public works construction and has built a turnover of £70M. It has a strong tradition of direct employment and is committed to the continuation of craft training programmes.

The company objectives

Typically the firm has economic and non-economic objectives. The economic objectives are to:

1. Consistently return a satisfactory and increasing annual net profit;
2. Achieve a satisfactory return on capital employed;
3. Maintain a positive cash flow at *all* times;
4. Expand the business relative to market opportunities and staff capabilities;
5. Obtain repeat orders on a negotiated basis;
6. Stay in business.

It must be noted that these economic objectives are vague and are only of real value to the company when quantified. Such data is naturally sensitive and the company did not wish to reveal the economic targets which it had set.

The company's non-economic objectives are to:

1. Train and develop staff to enable them to fulfil their potential;
2. Maintain a high level of business integrity with a strong element of service to clients;
3. Act as a responsible member of the community;
4. Enjoy what the firm does.

The overriding objective is to expand and this expansion strategy will be discussed further.

The planning process

The process of strategy formulation in the company is driven by market analyses. Periodically a small task force is assembled to review current strategy and appraise whether new strategic directives are required. It must be noted that this is not an annual process nor does it happen at regular intervals. The background to this method is in the conduct of market research. Market research was seen as important in the late 1970s to compare the quality of market information. The task force is charged with the task of assessing opportunities and options available to the firm in the context of the expected market for construction. The task force appraises the condition of the firm and matches the external opportunities with the capacity of the firm to take advantage of these opportunities. The task force then formulates a number of strategic options and presents these to the Board of Directors. The Board then opts for a particular strategy and oversees its implementation. Two themes have run through the strategic development of the company – growth and quality assurance. The growth strategy has been implemented by an expansion of the number of depots from two offices in 1977 to eight offices in 1987 throughout the region where it operates. This growth in the number of offices has meant that projects are supervised from a local administrative centre. Thus the growth has been matched by a level of decentralization of markets. From primary interests in property development the firm has developed into general contract work and has made inroads into design and build activities for industrial and retail clients. Using the model developed by Newcombe *et al.* (1990) the company has moved from a single dominant market to a related regional market. This is illustrated in Figure 7.1.

The key to the strategy for growth was to provide a quality service to clients. Consequently the company's strategy was to

	Single Market	Dominant in One Market	Related Diversification	Unrelated Diversification
Local firm	1970			
Regional firm			1989	
National firm				
International firm				

Figure 7.1 Company growth and market position

encourage repeat business by providing a construction service which was quality assured.

The planning process is fairly formal with the strategy emerging from research of market opportunities and market expectations of the services that contractors will be expected to provide in the 1990s. However, this process is driven by a small number of senior executives who then have a responsibility to carry out the strategy. As such this approach may be characterized as a 'top down' approach with little involvement of the operating units. Nonetheless the commitment of the local managers to the growth and quality strategy is evident and the strategy is communicated to managers. It would appear that the senior executives enjoy the confidence of their operating managers and the culture of training and development is one of the factors which cements the commitment to strategic objectives.

Conclusion

Several patterns of strategy formulation can be detected in these five case studies. They vary from being highly formalized to entrepreneurial, opportunistic and informal; from being collectively formulated to individually created. Three distinct approaches in the formulation of strategy can be detected:

1. The corporate approach in which managers of operating divisions are invited to construct a strategy for these divisions.
2. The 'wise man' approach in which a small sub-committee of senior managers creates a strategy and drives it through the company.
3. The creation of strategy by a single key figure of the company with assistance from corporate planners employed by the company or from consultants.

Using the dimensions of 'formality' and 'individuality' of strategy formulation a quarternion can be created as shown in Figure 7.2. It must be pointed out that the location of the companies within this grid is subjective; they are not positioned by measurements taken within the company. How-

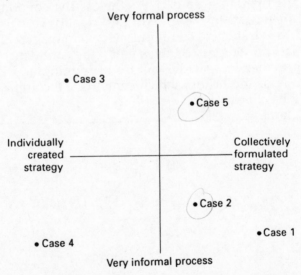

Figure 7.2   Case study patterns of strategy formulation

ever, the grid does illustrate that the more mature the company and the more diversified its services the greater the tendency for formality in the planning process.

It has not been the brief of this chapter to investigate the strategy of each company – this was a jealously guarded secret – but certain generic strategies can be detected from the research. Their strategies are consistent with the way in which strategy is formulated in the company. So the entrepreneurial firm makes strategy whilst the large conglomerate has a very much more bureaucratic approach. In general, in the larger organizations the process was more formalized and specialist staff advised the managers. In the less mature and smaller firms strategy was much more personal and depended upon the personality of key management figures rather than systems to implement the strategy.

Porter (1980) has noted that most firms adopt one of three generic strategies:

- Cost leadership;
- Differentiation; or
- Niche.

The case studies can be classified in this way. Case studies 1 and 2 provide examples of cost leadership with operating centres of the business providing services to clients competitively. Case studies 3 and 5 use differentiation strategy with design and build being a vehicle to differentiate the services provided by the company described in case study 3. The company depicted in case study 5 seeks differentiation by a strong commitment to apprentice training and by being in the forefront of the quality assurance movement. The company in case study 4 is an example of a firm which uses a niche strategy.

8

Strategic planning by professional consultants

Chapter 7 examined how construction companies develop and apply strategic management to their organizations. These concepts can, of course, be applied to consultants' organizations. Fresh managerial thinking has become part of the culture of many professional organizations during the growth of professional activities during the 1970s. Certainly the size of professional practices in construction has grown throughout the 1970s and 1980s and important new practices have emerged from amalgamations, mergers and takeovers. *Building* (15 September 1989) charted the growth of the professional sector. Not only have the sizes of firms grown (many of the practices listed in *Building* employed over 1000 staff) but the concerns of managers are focused upon strategic development of the organization. In part such developments have been fuelled by changes of structure in professional practices. Many have sought to change their status from partnerships to limited liability companies, some have sought flotations on the Unlisted Securities Market and surely some will seek promotion to a full Stock Exchange listing shortly. Such changes have also meant that the ownership of the practices has changed and for some large practices a considerable equity is held by financial institutions and financial services groups.

The changes in patterns of ownership may have meant that professional practices have been encouraged to formulate strategic plans and could be the reason for the trend towards strategic management. The process of strategic formulation within professional practices is illustrated by considering as case studies three professional consultancies.

CASE STUDY 1: A medium-sized quantity surveying practice

Background
This organization is a private practice which features in *Building*'s 'top 50 consultancy practices'. It is a very old established firm which comprises ten offices and over a hundred partners with staff involved in UK and overseas projects. The bulk of the firm's workload is in the South East but branch offices are scattered throughout the North and West. These branch offices were set up following commissions from existing or new clients.

The objectives of the practice
The stated objective of the practice is profit maximization. However, the practice recognizes a paradox in this objective: the practice states that it is client-orientated and exists to serve clients yet how can this co-exist with profit maximization? The objective of servicing client needs may create long-term stability by generating repeat orders but does not sit easily with profit maximization where a more overtly commercial approach may be deemed necessary. Notwithstanding this potential conflict the practice is currently extending its 'product range' by introducing project management services for existing clients. This could have the effect of increasing the size of assignments and the practice could be trusted with more responsibility for the building process.

The planning process
Typically, for professional practices, the planning process is left to senior partners. The tradition of the practice means that they frequently react to events by recognizing internal problems or an external opportunity as and when they arise. A good example of this planning process is the creation of new offices. The decision to open a branch office is driven by the invitation of clients to work in a particular location. In the period 1965–1971 the practice expanded into four new geographical locations not because it saw advantages in doing so but as a reaction to pressures from clients. This strategy has created difficulties as on more than one occasion a branch

office has been starved of work when clients shelved construction plans. This mode of planning could be said to be more
tactical than strategic: there seemed to be little systematic
approach to the geographical expansion.

This phase of responsive and reactive 'planning' was
replaced by a more proactive style in the early 1980s. The
retirement of some of the partners created space for a strategic
plan which sought to identify weaknesses of the practice and
to restructure to enable the practice better to fit the more
aggressive business climate of the 1980s. A number of changes
were introduced to the practice; amongst the more influential
was a separation of the professional functions of the practice
and the administration of the partnership. The partnership
administrator (appointed in 1988) not only has responsibility
for routine administration such as insurance, legal matters,
accounts and job costing, etc. but has a brief to develop
corporate strategy. This change in the planning process separ-
ates the business development of the practice from the routine
operational aspects of a quantity surveying practice. This
enables strategic thinking to take place and the partners to
implement the agreed plans. Since the appointment of a practice administrator the planning process has become more formalized. Strategic planning is undertaken by a management
committee which comprises the senior partner, two other
partners with an equity stake and the partnership administrator. The groundwork for strategic decisions is undertaken
by the partnership administrator. The strategic plan is then
presented to all partners. One consequence of this approach
is that task forces have been established to create policy and
drive it through the organization. Task forces have been
created for the following topics:

- Quality assurance systems
- Recruitment and training
- Marketing
- Information technology.

Conclusions
This practice is in the process of change from being a reactor
to events in the construction environment to one where considered strategic decisions are taken about the direction of the
partnership. This change has had implications for the structure of the practice. Previously each branch office dealt with
all aspects of the business but now there is a degree of special-

ization with only three of the ten offices dealing with project management commissions and a wholly-owned subsidiary dealing with quantity surveying in mechanical and electrical services. This specialization has meant that the earnings from conventional quantity surveying have fallen from 95 per cent in 1975 to 60 per cent in 1989. Project management fees represent some 40 per cent of fee income.

Such changes are a function of the movement to more formalized planning. It is perhaps inevitable that early experiments with strategic planning will tend to be 'top down' in that a small cohort of senior staff lower the plans on to the branch offices. The words used by the practice to describe the process of disseminating the plan are significant. The plan is 'presented to the partners for endorsement and implementation' not for discussion and revision. Nonetheless this is an interesting example of how concepts of strategic management can be applied to what could have been described in the 1970s as a very conventional quantity surveying practice.

CASE STUDY 2:   A large multi-disciplinary design practice

Background

The principal activity of this practice is the provision of design services to the construction industry. The practice began life in the late 1950s as an architectural practice but during the 1960s it sought to diversify so that all of the professional design disciplines (with the exception of quantity surveying) were employed to enable a broader range of work to be undertaken. It now has work which ranges from architecture, landscape architecture, interior design, project management and structural engineering to process engineering. The largest section of the portfolio in 1989 was 'retail' which accounted for about 33 per cent of the workload with commercial work representing 25 per cent and housing, of various types, constituting the remainder. The architectural side of the practice accounts for over 70 per cent of fee income. This income is drawn from the activity of eleven branch offices spread throughout the South of England. Each office is considered as a profit centre.

The practice took a bold step in the late 1980s to seek a flotation in the Unlisted Securities Market. Although share prices have fallen the company (née practice) is confident about its future and questions whether the financial markets have sufficient experience to accurately value a design company's share price.

The company objectives

In common with other design organizations the company publicly professes to have a strong commitment to quality. This commitment is expressed in the company literature and the route to high quality design is seen as the recruiting of high quality staff. This concern for quality is embedded in a mission statement of the company. This mission statement emphasizes the importance of satisfying clients in terms of quality of product as well as in terms of the time and costs incurred during the construction process. This approach is pressed home by periodic quality reviews and slogans such as 'Nothing breeds success like a quality service'.

A more tangible objective of the company is the stated aim of risk spreading. The company firmly adheres to the policy of remaining general practitioners to avoid a dependence on any one client or sector of the industry. This objective is made operational by seeking a relatively large number of smaller commissions to ensure that work is spread across the industry. Apart from the issue of project portfolio management the organization has to recognize its status as a public company and consequently has economic objectives. The company operates each office as a profit centre and managers have the financial objective of a minimum of 20 per cent profit on capital employed. The organization met its targets in 1988 and 1989 and was able to offer modest increases in the earnings per share although the yield for shareholders is relatively poor.

The planning process

The company carries out a formal process of self-appraisal by periodically preparing a SWOT analysis. The objective of this analysis is to appraise past performance and seek areas for future improvement. The strategic 'think-tank' is the main Board of Directors headed by an executive chairman. This Board consists of nine persons: the chairman, deputy chair, the finance director and a non-executive director comprise the executive committee, and there are five regional directors. This group is responsible for the formulation and monitoring of the implementation of strategy. After a strategy is formed it is discussed with the regional Board for comment and discussion of how it can be put into operation.

The strategy of going public was obviously controversial and it was predicated on the basis that expansion was the key to corporate success. The problem was analysed and although organic, internally generated growth was seen as desirable it was too slow to ensure improvements and extensions of the services offered to clients. The company chose an acquisition route to expand the client base and to diversify the professional skills held by the firm and its geographical area of operations. Funds made available from the flotation were also used to provide a state of the art computer-aided design set up and to acquire related businesses. The process of creating such strategy may be defined as top down but the strategy is informed and refined by information provided by the operating firms.

Conclusions

The company has used a formal planning process to change the culture of the organization from one driven by professional values to one which retains a core of professional conduct but operates in a commercial and businesslike fashion. The strategy adopted is bold and is a response to the environment which encouraged the creation of larger business units during the 1980s. Without a formal plan it is doubtful if the achievement of the company would have been realized.

CASE STUDY 3:   A progressive quantity surveying practice

Background

This practice is a large quantity surveying practice with head offices in the North of England and nineteen branch offices, some of which are based overseas. The company has developed from a traditional quantity surveying practice to one which offers specialized services to specific market sectors. The company dates from the late 1940s but it was during the 1960s and 1970s that the firm developed expertise in quantity surveying services for process and industrial engineering, and although this market has declined the expertise gained in this area enabled the practice to generate work in the building construction aspects of surveying. In common with many other surveying practices it saw diversification as necessary to enable it to develop and be synchronized with a rapidly changing external environment. Consequently the firm offers services which range from preparation of tender documents to feasibility studies and life cycle costing. More recently project management services and quantity surveying for mechanical and electrical services have been added to the workload of the practice.

Objective

The stated objective is organizational growth. The practice has sought to grow by a combination of internally generated growth and passive acquisition. This growth has resulted in the size of the organization, in terms of number of employees, being more than doubled in the period 1975–1989. Such growth was coupled with some restructuring; a small group of four partners forms the senior management team and the middle management is staffed by partners who direct the work of each branch office.

The planning process

Prior to 1984 the firm had a reactive style of strategic development. Frequently new offices were opened in response to the promise of an existing client to provide work on a development in a particular part of the country. There is other evidence of this 'reactor' approach; in an interview one of the partners revealed a strong opportunistic streak. If the partners saw a business opportunity in the market then they would 'go for it', seemingly mindful that the previously agreed strategy had not identified the opportunity as an arena for their business development. This opportunistic approach is, however, tempered by a formalized strategic planning process. The senior management formally meet once every two months to review progress on the implementation of strategy. Strategy is formulated by this group with the assistance of a development division of the practice. This division, based at the head office, has a primary role of considering organizational development. Changes in direction of strategy appear to emanate from this division and papers are presented for discussion by senior management. Therefore the strategic planning process has become much more formal.

Discussion of strategy is not accepted as part of the responsibilities of the branch offices. These units have to implement the chosen strategy and the practice recognizes that it is autocratic in its management style as policy is lowered on to these offices. However, the practice is cognisant of potential problems and a strong social life is fostered within the practice and formal communications through newsletters, etc. provide the necessary sustenance to keep the staff loyal.

Conclusions

Financial data was not available for review but the impression given was that the practice was active and progressive. The process of strategy formulation has moved from being reactive to a mixture of reactive and proactive and this fusion of entrepreneurialism and structured organizational development keeps the practice dynamic yet stable. This curious combination means that growth has occurred in an organic and a planned way; the question is whether this coalition of planning styles can sustain the relatively high morale amongst staff given the relatively centralized basis for formal strategic planning.

Conclusion

The case studies of consultants' practices cannot be assimilated as easily as those of construction organizations. The first problem is that the number of practices willing to offer information was insufficient to enable any trends to be determined and further, the quality of information available does little to illuminate the field of strategic management in consulting practices. In part this is due to the maturity of the practices as strategic business clients. Those few practices which have become limited liability companies have not had time to develop in scope of activity or size to consider the various models of strategic management. However, some common threads can be seen, albeit these are tentative observations rather than conclusions.

First the preferred style of strategic formulation is strongly entrepreneurial and opportunistic. A small group of partners who create the strategy and lower it onto branch offices was the common style of strategy formulation. In all three examples this strategy involved aspects of geographical decentralization by the opening up of branch offices in other areas of the country. However, this growth was seldom 'planned' but more often was at the behest of regular clients. A second common feature was related diversification. As practices grew from local organizations into those with regional or national presence there was a tendency to offer specialized services (such as project management) with particular offices dealing with the specialist commissions. Two of the three practices could be termed 'passive acquirers' (Channon 1978) in that they sought to buy out other practices to become diversified in the services they offered clients. Finally all three practices were seen to emphasize quality of service as a key instrument in attracting and holding clients. Two of the practices had some form of internal quality assurance scheme but none had moved as far as seeking certification under the British Standard (BS 5754) quality assurance scheme.

It is difficult to place the consultancy practices within the framework of Porter's (1980) generic strategies (see p. 40). Certainly none of those surveyed sought to attract clients by competing on the price of service, nor could the services be seen as highly differentiated because of the similarities of the professional roles and the uniformity of the professional standards expected by professional institutions such as RIBA and RICS. However, a small element of differentiation could be detected in the combinations of services provided to clients, the amount of technology that was applied to projects and the proximity of a branch office to the client's project. Only a niche strategy remains and although the evidence is weak it may be suggested that there is a small element of niche strategy being applied. Each practice seeks to focus upon new services which provide a niche in the market. However, the skill of 'nichemanship' is to recognize gaps in the market and seek competitive advantage by being early to service those niches. The practices could not really be seen to approach their markets in this way: none of the practices had prepared market maps to discover what, if any, service was required by the market which it was not being offered. Thus all three practices have intuitively gauged project management services as being a good future prospect. The two practices which grew out of quantity surveying have extended their range of services by offering specialist services for mechanical and electrical services. However, it is recognized that this action does not really fit a niche strategy, it merely suggests that market intelligence was read in the same way by the three firms.

It is clear that more research into the strategy process is required by consulting firms in the construction industry. At this stage it can be said that all the practices sense that corporate strategy is an important element in the management of their practices. With the exception of case study 1, where strategic advice was the responsibility of the administrator, the senior partners appear to be the key people involved in strategy and do not seek outside assistance in analysing the fit between the construction environment and the profile of the practice. However, the three practices are aware of the importance of strategic management and may seek to refine its formulation and implementation as they become more marginally sophisticated and as their culture changes from a professional culture with emphasis upon individual and excellent service to clients to one which is driven by commercial values.

9

A synthesis of strategy management in construction

The primary aims of this book are to develop the concepts of strategy in the construction industry, both corporate – concerned with the whole firm – and business – concerned with competition in particular markets, and the process of strategic decision-making and how this can shift the boundary of the firm in relation to its external business environment. This chapter brings together the earlier themes of the book and synthesizes them to raise some implications for strategic management in construction. It concludes with a contingency model of strategic management for the construction industry.

The construction industry can be characterized as a series of overlapping markets in terms of size, geographic location, type and complexity of project. Within this market structure demand is biased towards the private sector. There has been a long-term decline in public sector investment and the shift towards the private sector and the increasingly speculative nature of demand, especially in the commercial, industrial and housing sectors, implies that there will be a need for contractors to make greater investments in land banks. As a consequence of the amounts of capital required to be tied up in land or property – as fixed assets – contractors will not be able to enjoy in the future the flexibility they have enjoyed in the past. Additionally, the construction market is currently dominated by the South of England. A distinct geographical imbalance has emerged tempered by pockets of active development in other parts of the country. Furthermore, with an increase in the number of smaller projects, contractors will have to bid on and manage more projects in order to maintain turnover. The net effect will be an increase in the number of managerial grades within construction companies. There is a consequential implication for both overheads and profits. Previous chapters have argued that profitability in the industry is affected by the general level of economic activity, with long-term changes in demand evidenced as sectoral shifts in market structure. These effects are working through the collective business environments of buyers (or clients) to the industry. With these long-term shifts in markets, especially the increase in repair and maintenance work, the move towards smaller project sizes in some market sectors will necessitate different work patterns, skills and training requirements.

Environmental change and the strategic behaviour of contractors

The environment of the construction industry has gone through a series of evolutionary changes since the Second World War. These changes can be characterized as operational, strategic and competitive. Firms, as economic and social entities, have the capacity to learn from and adapt to environmental changes. Adaptation occurs through the exercise, by senior managers, of strategic choice. Additionally, depending on size, firms have the capacity to influence their environments to a certain extent – a prime example being the use of professional lobbyists to government or recruiting Members of Parliament to act as non-executive members on a company's Board of Directors. Each type of environmental condition requires of senior managers not only the ability to be able to read signals of different strengths but also to utilize different skills in order to respond to environmental pressure in an appropriate manner.

Operational changes in the environment, characteristic of the 1950s and 1960s, allow managers to concentrate their efforts on raising internal efficiencies. The strategic management process under this type of environmental condition is relatively simple and senior managers can formulate strategies based on experience. Strategic behaviour will be based on incrementalism and a predominant bias towards an internal orientation. However, a watchful eye should be maintained for changes in the external environment. The danger under these conditions is that senior managers' attention will only focus internally to the exclusion of environmental scanning. Under this type of environmental condition there is likely to be a high incidence of the defender type of firm.

Strategic changes in the environment, characteristic of the late 1960s and 1970s, are dramatic, discontinuous and unfamiliar. The important point with this type of environmental condition is the high rate of change. Firms need to maintain flexibility. There is likely to be a number of strategic options available in construction under these conditions, for example, divestment, retrenchment and expansion into new markets, either internally or through acquisition. Firms will exhibit different types of strategic behaviour, for example, those firms with a full corporate strategic capability which can be utilized to its maximum benefit are more likely to follow a proactive systematic planning mode. Those firms with a less complete form of strategic capability are likely to follow a proactive ad hoc mode of behaviour. However, firms taken unawares by such drastic changes in their environment will follow a reactive mode. Under conditions of strategic environmental change senior managers will require creative insight, and will need to focus their attention on the external business environment and understand their employees' concerns about external changes and the possible impact on the firm. Senior managers will require, therefore, an orientation that is both corporate, external and people-oriented. Under such environmental conditions it is likely that there will be a preponderance of prospector, analyser and reactor types in the industry.

Under conditions of competitive change, characteristic of the 1980s and early 1990s, the environment will exhibit attributes that have elements of strategic and operational change. Demand is unpredictable but rates of change are not as drastic as under conditions of strategic change. It could be argued that under such conditions the skill requirements of senior managers are greatest since management in this type of climate requires a combination of, and hence effective integration of, both creative insight and experience. Strategic behaviour will favour proactive systematic or ad hoc modes. The industry is likely to have a high incidence of prospectors and analysers with limited defender capabilities due to the unpredictability of demand and the subsequent dangers from over specialization as sectoral or sub-market demand shifts.

The construction industry comprises firms that differ by

type, size and scope of work. Within both contracting and the professions there has been a restructuring of firm sizes biased either towards the larger or smaller firms. The natural consequence of this is that the medium-sized firm is under increasing competitive pressure from both ends of the size scale. Contracting firms differ in size and business scope, some operating within the local vicinity whilst others operate regionally, nationally or internationally. The degree of geographic business scope of a contracting firm will set the competitive arena in terms of markets and sub-markets within which it operates and the competitors that the firm will face. Contracting firms can be differentiated with reference to those that undertake to build the physical product, using domestic or sub-contracted labour, in comparison to those that provide a management service only and therefore extensively use subcontractors. Contracting can be defined, therefore, in terms of discreet international markets where some firms provide a service and others have the characteristics of a manufacturing operation. Different parts of a contracting firm tackle different sub-markets and the concept of the strategic business unit has direct application in dealing with the strategic management of such a diversity of operational business environments. The use of the principles of portfolio management techniques also has considerable application. In the face of increasing uncertainty in their business environments, contractors are spreading their risks by strategies of related diversification into connected markets.

Environmental change and the strategic behaviour of consultants

The professional consultants in construction can be broken down into two broad groups: designers, namely, architects and the different specialisms within the engineering profession; and surveyors, also of different specialisms. For a variety of historical, status and competitive reasons the construction professions are now facing intra- and inter-professional competitive rivalry.

The effects of the industry environment vary according to the size of the consultancy. In the architectural profession the larger offices employ most of the staff and carry out the greatest volume of work. These firms also deal with corporate clients, both public and private, although changes in government policy have decreased the volume of work from the former. The large architectural practices have a portfolio of buildings that are heavily biased towards commercial and industrial property or undertake feasibility studies. With the increasing pressure from clients for one-stop-shopping, architectural practices are forming strategic alliances, either formally or informally, to provide multi-disciplinary services. Large consultancy practices will have a more stable clientele, are more involved in the strategic end of projects and have in the past been forced by client demands into specialization by project type. Small practices are dominated by private-sector clients, with increased variability in workload and have also been forced to specialize due to client demand. The medium-sized practices, under pressure from industry restructuring, which favours the small and large practices, will have to make considerable strategic choices if they are to survive. Evidence from general practice surveying indicates that the options for the medium-sized firm are for growth through internal expansion or acquisition. However, the ramifications of such a strategy involve resources, especially access to capital, the presence of strategic management skills among senior managers and the overall staff capability to handle change. Competitive fee bidding may force a move away from specialization to a generalist orientation.

As a result of competition from the surveying profession, the emerging project management approach, client pressure and perhaps personal or corporate choice, architects appear to be focusing more on design at the expense of breadth of involvement in the building/construction process. Client commercial pressures in terms of greater requirements for financial, cost, legal and management control of the building process – areas where architects, for example, are under considerable threat from the surveyors – are likely to exaggerate the shift towards design for architectural and engineering consultants. Coupled with this fact is the allied situation that, for example, in the case of quantity surveying, it is the leading edge of that profession which is taking on board the more innovative services. However, in terms of strategic management capabilities, evidence from the general practice surveying field indicates that there is an over concentration on operational planning at the expense of strategic planning. This suggests a strategic orientation of incrementalism. This, in conjunction with the fact that since the early 1980s professional consultant markets have moved towards deregulation and hence a free market situation, means that many firms are facing at least competitive if not strategic change. The evidence to support such a contention is found in the increased use of sub-contracting in consultancy firms, a strategy used to cope with workload fluctuations. Additional evidence supports the move towards strategic change for consultants by the fact that clients are becoming increasingly less interested in the *means* by which professionals achieve results – that is, the form that skills take – but are becoming *ends* or *results* oriented. Clients are blurring the distinctions between professional and commercial services. This is a significant move away from the traditional business environments that the professions have had to respond to in the past. The probable outcome for professional organization will be a change in organizational form towards commercial as opposed to professional organization. Many consultancy firms will find this transition and its implications difficult to make or appreciate.

The distinction between organizational forms under professional versus commercial dominance is elaborated below with reference to Mintzberg's (1979) typology. However, in brief it is concerned with the degree of shift away from, or balance between, skills acquired through external institutions – the professional bureaucracy – versus those acquired internally – the machine bureaucracy. The ramifications for skills transferability within professions and between firms can become considerable over time.

An analysis of the case studies

The case studies of contracting firms highlighted a number of significant issues for strategic management in construction. First, the international contractor had a formalized strategic management process with a long-term time horizon of ten to fifteen years. Subsequently, a series of integrated short-term operational plans of either one or two years were utilized. This company combined both 'top down' and 'bottom up' procedures in the strategic formulation process. Second, the small national design and build contractor operated in both a general mode, through its management contracting division, and a niche mode through its design and build operations. The strategic management process can best be described as 'top down', autocratic and opportunistic. The firm has utilized retrenchment strategies. It is moving from an informal strategic management process to a more formalized approach with the appointment of a corporate planner. This appears to have been stimulated by potentially damaging signs in the firm's private sector dominated business environment. The third example, the regional civil engineering company, faced a number of important issues, such as, bad debts, retrenchment from overseas activities and subsequent moves into other international markets, an unsuccessful move into management contracting and the creation of a development company, and these forced a reappraisal of the company's activities and a realignment of the business scope of the firm. The company has now adopted a formal approach to the strategic management process with SWOT analyses and a two-year strategic plan and shorter-term operating plans. The study of the regional SBU of a national contracting group revealed a strategic planning system that can best be described as ad hoc systematic. In this instance a task force is utilized periodically to formulate a series of strategic options for the Board of Directors to consider. The strategic management process is, therefore, 'top down' and partially formalized. The medium-sized residential developer considered in case study 5 was market niche-oriented and had to instigate a retrenchment strategy when their market sector niche experienced a slump in demand. The strategic management process was 'top down', entrepreneurial with the use of outside consultants for market research.

For the consultancy practice case studies the following picture emerges. First, the development of the medium-sized quantity surveying practice was heavily influenced by client pressure in the setting up of branch offices. The decision to open such offices was not a premeditated strategic decision. It was, therefore, an operational or tactical decision. In the event, this caused problems for the firm when client workloads eased up and branch offices had periods of work famine. A change in the senior management team provided an opportunity for a strategic re-evaluation of the firm. As a consequence, a distinction was made between professional and administrative areas within the firm. The partnership administrator then became responsible for generating the corporate plan and the partners took over responsibility for implementation. The strategic management process can be described as formalized and 'top down'. The second quantity surveying practice could be characterized as reactive until the mid-1980s. It has now moved to an opportunistic strategic management process tempered by some formality with the process again being 'top down'. The firm has opted for growth either through internal expansion or passive acquisition. Finally, the multi-disciplinary design practice is in a different situation from the previous two consultancies in that it is a quoted firm on the USM. This firm has a formal strategic management process in operation including the presence of mission statements and quantifiable objectives. However, the process could best be described as an ad hoc systematic approach with formal SWOT analyses undertaken periodically. The strategists are the main Board of Directors. The strategic management process is 'top down' but modified by 'bottom up' procedures. The firm is actively pursuing a diversification strategy to broaden both its skills and client base. It is therefore using the notion of the project portfolio for strategic development. In addition, this particular firm has opted for SBUs that are profit rather than cost centres and has introduced an entrepreneurial dimension into its operations.

Strategic typologies revisited

A number of typologies have been put forward for describing firms in the construction industry. Reference has been made to some of these throughout the preceding paragraphs. However, the typology suggested by Mintzberg (1979) is useful in moving towards the implications for strategic management in construction and this is outlined below.

Simple structure

This structure is endemic in the construction industry. It is typified by minimal structure and is organic. The problem for this organizational type is that the operating and strategic decision-making processes often become intermixed and overlap. As a result of organizational size, the strategic management process, if present in any identifiable form, will probably be incremental, short term and reactive. The simple structure characterizes many sub-contracting firms.

Simple professional structure

This structure is characteristic of the small consultancy organization. Small architectural practices have been identified as being highly organic. This stems from the fact that they face environments that are dynamic because of the volatility of workloads.

Professional bureaucracies

As consultancy firms become larger the emergence of this structure occurs where the emphasis for the production level is on standardized skills. This structure typifies the medium and large consultancy firms prior to the removal of scales of fees. In this respect, the environments faced by these firms were relatively predictable since they were likely to have a more stable clientele and revenue generation was controlled. However, due to the introduction of competitive fee bids and the fact that client pressures are changing, the professional bureaucracy may give way to a number of different structural forms in the professions. In this instance the pull by market forces could be towards ad hocracy or machine bureaucracy depending on the degree of personal services or technology emphasized in the production core and the degree to which the control over standardization is internally or externally generated. However, the important point is that for consultancy firms moving away from the professional bureaucratic form the strategic management process would be different in each case. For the consultancy firm investing heavily in technology to gain a competitive edge, for example through computer-based billing or integrated computer-aided design and billing, the strategic management process would favour the systematic planning mode to enable the firm to keep abreast of technological developments. For the consultancy firm moving towards ad hocracy, where the emphasis is on a personalized client-oriented service, the emphasis would favour the systematic ad hoc mode.

Depending on their size, construction firms will have the most complex structural forms in terms of Mintzberg's typology. The large, multiple SBU construction organizations have a divisional structure. However, the nature of each division will be different. For example, in those construction companies with divisions which cover building materials (machine bureaucracy), property development and project management (professional bureaucracy/adhocracy) and contracting (ad hocracy), the strategic management process becomes one of managing divisional interdependences and disparities between market structures. As organizational size and market diversity decrease the push is towards simple structure with overlays of other structural forms.

Futures and the development of strategies

The tracing of the environmental evolution of the construction industry since the Second World War has highlighted the fact that familiarization of present and future environments is assisted by a formal strategic planning process and the development of a clear vision of the future direction of the firm, its objectives and a set of strategies to meet those objectives. Chapter 4, which looked at futures, highlighted the fact that underpinning this work is uncertainty and a philosophy of change. Ansoff (1987) has argued that under a given set of environmental conditions a range of strategic behaviours are possible. The message that we would like to convey is that regardless of the size of a firm, strategic decisions can be made that increase the degree of 'fit' between the firm and its business environment and hence improve its chance of survival. The examination of futures highlighted three fundamental questions that can be addressed regardless of firm size. To reiterate, these were:

- What choices do I have? This question focuses the mind on constraints and associated resource implications. Again, this has to take account of organizational politics.
- What do I know? This question firmly addresses the current knowledge base of the firm. SWOT analysis is one technique that could address this issue of a firm's capabilities.
- What do I prefer? Preferences usually involve some political consequences within organizations.

The size of firm will obviously have an impact on the degree to which futures work can subsequently be used. For example, the use of models, traces or analysis of witnesses to create alternative possible futures would be beyond the scope of many organizations within construction. However, this does not negate the principles upon which it is based. For example, the Board of Directors of a medium-sized contracting or consultancy firm could generate a series of possible futures based on their own knowledge of the industry. The choice of perhaps a couple of probable futures would sensitize senior management to a range of issues that the firm may not have considered. If a series of alternative strategies are developed for these probable futures, the firm has moved towards second generation or contingency planning. The problem associated with exploring and examining possibilities, which the implementation of futures work entails, is that it involves threats and challenges to existing ways of thinking and modes of behaviour. There is no reason why a 'futures' type of analysis could not be undertaken in either the systematic planning or systematic ad hoc modes. The case studies have highlighted the fact that a number of strategic behaviours are in evidence. The large international contractor operates a formalized systematic planned approach. As one moves down the size category of firms, the degree of formality and regularity of the strategic management process varies. There is also a preponderance of 'top down' processes. It must be added that the case studies are examples and generalization is not easily possible from them. It can be postulated, however, based on the empirical studies highlighted in Chapters 7 and 8 and discussed in more detail above, that the overriding strategic approach within construction appears to be one of incrementalism, predominantly based on operational thinking. Within some construction and consultancy organizations there is now a move towards a systematic ad hoc mode and within a few large companies a systematic planned mode has been adopted.

Strategic flexibility

The generation of alternative courses of action, or as the review of futures work has suggested, of alternative possible futures, will facilitate flexibility. The key issue is that a firm's senior managers, as the strategic decision-makers, have a crucial role to play in shaping the flexible firm. Of the five criteria isolated and suggested by Lansley *et al.* (1979) for strategic flexibility, three are directly related to the actions of senior management and the other two stem from such action, with their effects being felt by employees. Lansley (1987) has recently suggested that the environments of the late 1980s and early 1990s require responses from firms that are more task-oriented with less emphasis on people orientation. This suggests, using Clark's (1989) notion of repertoires of multiple structures, that the contracting firms of the 1990s will need not only to rediscover some of their latent organizational structures of the late 1960s and 1970s but also to integrate these in order to produce organizational structures and strategic responses capable of handling the attributes of the competitive environments of the decade. Additionally, as the 1990s unfold in terms of national government policies, as the implications of the single European market become more clear and as the opportunities and/or threats of the monumental events in Eastern Europe crystalize, construction companies may have to rediscover organizational repertoires relevant to strategic change. The crux of this analysis is that the construction industry is heavily dependant on human capital. In practice this means, for a firm: the knowledge possessed by the organization, either by people or codified and written down in documents, the ability of the organization to learn from the past and present to allow it to take action for the future, the skill base of the firm and the level of investment in training and managerial development, and finally the extent to which the skill base of the firm is eroded as people leave. Based on the present assessment, therefore, strategic management in construction for the 1990s requires a combination of both corporate and operational planning.

A contingency model of strategic management for construction

As an introduction to this model an example can be taken of how Porter's (1980) framework can be used for analysing the industry pressures on an individual consultancy organization. Figure 9.1 sets out the forces facing a hypothetical quantity surveying firm. The basic framework has been modified using the additional variable – stakeholders. This variable to the framework is useful in a construction context since, depending on the nature of the firm studied, stakeholders are active as a competitive force within the construction industry. By using this framework as an analytical tool strategists can focus their attention on the key influences on the firm. These in turn can be aggregated to analyse the overall impact on costs

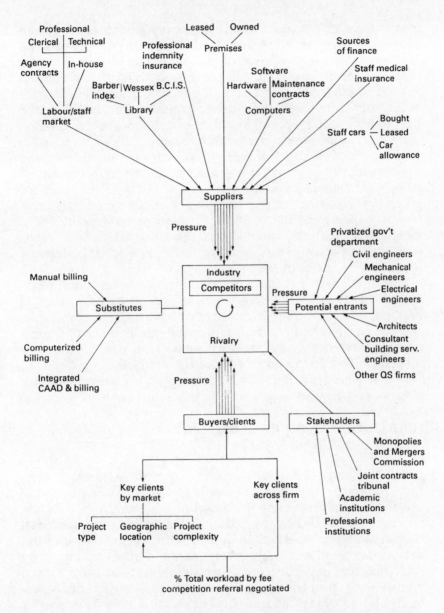

Figure 9.1 Competitive forces analysis: a quantity surveying firm

Source: adapted from *Competitive Strategy*. Porter (1980)

and subsequently profits. For example, by analysing key clients within existing markets and then aggregating these to company level, attention is directed away from business strategy – competing in individual markets – to the corporate level and the contingent impact of the potential loss of any one client on the total organization can be highlighted. Additionally, by highlighting aggregated client purchasing mechanisms at the corporate level – through fee competition, referrals and negotiation – it is possible to assess the degree of market variability and hence uncertainty facing the firm. A pilot analysis by Male using this framework for a consultancy and contracting organization has revealed that an in-depth analysis of the business environment within which a firm operates, given that construction is a fragmented industry, can generate considerable amounts of data. The important point for a meaningful analysis, having generated the data, is to focus only on those key factors that are important for the strategic operation of the firm.

Figure 9.2 sets out the basic framework of the contingency model of strategic management in construction, drawing together the important issues from each chapter. The model can be used as the first step in the strategic analysis of a firm, making reference to the relevant sections in each chapter for understanding the components of the analysis. The depth to which the analysis is taken depends very much on the size of firm and the resources available for the analysis.

Organizational repertoires

In conclusion, Clark (1989), using empirical research, asserts that large firms in particular have repertoires of multiple structures. The analysis of the evolution of the construction industry since the 1950s has suggested that different environmental conditions have emerged, requiring different responses from senior managers and their organizations. Firms, having faced such different environmental conditions, would have stored within their collective experience different structural repertoires. Some organizational structures would lie dormant for long periods of time to re-emerge when required by forces within the environment and/or within the firm. Lansley (1987) has argued that as a consequence of a long-term downturn in economic activity there are environmental pressures on firms to rationalize and hence adopt innovation and new value systems ready for the next upswing in economic activity. His analysis and that undertaken for this book would

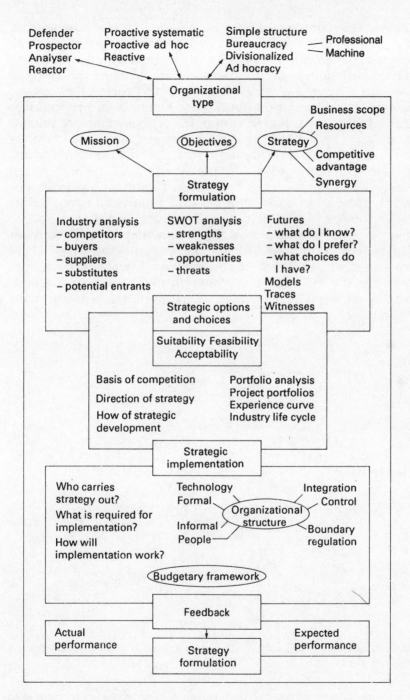

Figure 9.2 A contingency model of strategic management

Source: Porter, *Competitive Strategy* (1980)

suggest that contractors have to rediscover and combine their organizational repertoires of the 1960s and 1970s to produce a structure capable of handling competitive change. For contractors, therefore, the business environment of the 1990s is likely to require a strategic management process that is capable of concentrating on developing methods and procedures that promote the integration of both corporate and operational planning. The task facing consultancy organizations is different. Until the early 1980s their business environments were, to some extent, relatively predictable in revenue terms through the operation of fee scales. However, with deregulation, changes in client attitudes and an environment becoming increasingly speculative and private sector dominated, many of their organizational repertoires may be inappropriate for current conditions. Whilst the implantation of strategic management processes in construction firms is crucial, the need for professional consultancy firms to embrace the concept of strategic management for the 1990s is even more imperative.

Bibliography

Aldrich, H.E. (1979) *Organizations and Environments*, Prentice Hall, Englewood Cliffs: New Jersey.

Amara, R. (1975) *Some Methods of Future Research*, Institute for the Future: Menlo Park, California.

Ansoff, I. (1987) *Corporate Strategy*, 2nd edn, Penguin: Harmondsworth.

Avis, M.R. and V.A. Gibson (1987) *The Management of General Practice Surveying Firms*, Research Papers in Land Management and Development – Management, No. 1, March, University of Reading.

Ball, M. (1988) *Rebuilding Construction. Economic Change in the British Construction Industry*, Routledge: London.

Ball, M. and A. Cullen (1980) *Mergers and Accumulation in the British Construction Industry 1960–1979*, Birkbeck Discussion Paper No. 73, Birkbeck College: London.

Building Research Unit (1972) *Efficiency and Growth in the Building Industry*, Ashridge Management College.

Catherwood, F. (1966) 'Development and Organisation of Richard Costain' in R. Edwards and H. Townsend (eds) *Business Growth*, Macmillan: London.

Channon, D.F. (1978) *The Service Industries: Strategy, Structure and Financial Performance*, Macmillan: London.

Child, J. (1972) 'Organisational Structure, Environment and Performance: The Role of Strategic Choice', *Sociology*, **6**, pp. 1–22.

Clark, P. (1989) 'Social Technology and Structure' in P.M. Hillebrandt and J. Cannon (eds) *The Management of Construction Firms: Aspects of Theory*, Macmillan: Basingstoke.

Department of the Environment (1987) *Housing: The Government's Proposals*, Cmnd 214, HMSO: London.

Department of the Environment (1989) *Housing and Construction Statistics*, HMSO: London.

Fleming, M.C. (1988) 'Construction' in P. Johnson (ed.) *The Structure of British Industry*, 2nd edn, Unwin Hyman: London.

Grinyer, P. (1972) 'Systematic Strategic Planning for Construction Firms', *Building Technology and Management*, February, pp. 8–14.

Hillebrandt, P.J. (1984) *Analysis of the British Construction Industry*, Macmillan: London.

Hillebrandt, P.J. and Cannon, J. (1990) *The Modern Construction Firm*, Macmillan: Basingstoke.

Hillier, W. (1979) 'The Structure of the Profession Study'. Unpublished report for the Royal Institute of British Architects, Bartlett School of Architecture and Planning, University College: London.

Howe, W.S. (1986) *Corporate Strategy*, Macmillan: London.

Hunt, J.W. (1972) *The Restless Organisation*, John Wiley and Sons: Milton, Queensland.

Jauch, L.R. and W.F. Glueck (1988) *Business Policy and Strategic Management*, 5th edn, McGraw-Hill: Singapore.

de Jouvenal, B. (1967) *The Art of Conjecture*, Basic Books: New York.

Kast, F.E. and J.E. Rosenzweig (1981) 'The Modern View: A Systems Approach' in Open Systems Group (eds) *Systems Behaviour*, 3rd edn, Harper and Row: London.

Kaye, B. (1960) *The Development of the Architectural Profession in Britain*, Allen and Unwin: London.

Kelly, J.R. and S.P. Male (1987) *A Study of Value Engineering and Quantity Surveying Practice*, Final Report, March, Quantity Surveying Division, Royal Institute of Chartered Surveyors: London.

Lansley, P. (1987) 'Corporate Strategy and Survival in the UK Construction Industry', *Construction Management and Economics*, **5**, pp. 141–55.

Lansley, P. and T. Quince (1981) 'Organisational Responses to a Major Recession', *Construction Papers*, **1**(2), pp. 5–16.

Lansley, P., T. Quince and E. Lea (1979) *Flexibility and Efficiency in Construction Management*, Final Report, Building Industry Group, Ashridge Management College.

MAC (1985) *Competition and the Chartered Surveyor: Changing Client Demand for the Services of the Chartered Surveyor*, Report by Management Analysis Centre for the Royal Institution of Chartered Surveyors: London.

McNamee, P.B. (1985) *Tools and Techniques for Strategic Management*, Pergamon: Oxford.

Male, S.P. (1984) 'A Critical Investigation of Professionalism in Quantity Surveying'. Unpublished PhD thesis, Heriot-Watt University: Scotland.

Male, S.P. 'Professional Authority, Power and Emerging Forms of "Profession" in Quantity Surveying', *Construction Management and Economics*, v. 8, 1990, pp. 191–204.

Male, S.P. and J.R. Kelly (1989) 'The Organisational Responses of Two Public Sector Client Bodies in Canada and the Implementation Process of Value Management: Lessons for the UK Construction Industry', *Construction Management and Economics*, 7(3), pp. 203–16.

Male, S.P. and R. Stocks (1989) 'Managers and the Organisation' in P.M. Hillebrandt and J. Cannon (eds) *The Management of Construction Firms: Aspects of Theory*, Macmillan: Basingstoke.

Miles, R.E. and C.C. Snow (1978) *Organisational Strategy, Structure and Process*, McGraw-Hill: Tokyo.

Mintzberg, H. (1973) *The Nature of Managerial Work*, Harper and Row: New York.

Mintzberg, H. (1979) *The Structuring of Organizations*, Prentice Hall: Englewood Cliffs, New Jersey.

Monopolies and Mergers Commission (1977) *Architects Services*, HMSO: London.

Morrell, D. (1987) *Indictment: Power and Politics in the Construction Industry*, Faber and Faber: London.

NEDO (1988) *Construction Forecasts 1988, 1989, 1990*, HMSO: London.

Newcombe, R. (1976) 'The Evolution and Structure of the Construction Firm'. Unpublished MSc thesis, University College: London.

Newcombe, R., D. Langford and R. Fellows (1990) *Construction Management: A Systems Approach: Management Systems*, Batsford: London.

PRS (1987) *The Architect in a Competitive Market*, Report by Property Research Services for the Cities of London and Westminster Society of Architects and the London Region of the Royal Institute of British Architects: London.

Porter, M.E. (1980) *Competitive Strategy: Techniques for Analysing Industries and Competitors*, Free Press: New York.

RICS (1984) *A Study of Quantity Surveying Practice and Client Demand*, Report for the Quantity Surveyors Division, Royal Institution of Chartered Surveyors, Surveyors Publications: London.

Ramsey, W. (1989) 'Business Objectives' in P.M. Hillebrandt and J. Cannon (eds) *The Management of Construction Firms: Aspects of Theory*, Macmillan: Basingstoke.

Robbins, S.P. (1983) *Organization Theory: The Structure and*

Design of Organizations, Prentice Hall: Englewood Cliffs, New Jersey.

Taylor, B. and Sparkes, J. (1982) *Corporate Strategy and Planning*, Heinemann: London.

Usdiken, B., Z. Sozen and H. Enbiyaoglu (1987) *Strategies and Boundaries: Subcontracting in Construction*, CIB W–65 Discussion Paper, November.

Wheelan, J.D. and T.L. Hunger (1987) *Strategic Management*, 2nd edn, Addison-Wesley: Reading, Mass.

Wilson, I. (1978) 'Scenarios' in J. Fowles (ed.) *Handbook of Future Research*, Greenwood Press: California.

Zentner, A. (1975) 'Scenarios in Forecasting', *Chemical and Engineering News,* 6 October, pp. 22–35.

Index